GET CLOSER

A
DEVOTIONAL
FOR
ENCOUNTERING
GOD

Copyright © 2022 by Van Moody

Published by Kudu

All rights reserved. No portion of this book may be reproduced, stored in a retrieval system, or transmitted in any form or by any means—electronic, mechanical, photocopy, recording, scanning, or other—except for brief quotations in critical reviews or articles, without prior written permission of the author.

Scripture quotations marked NIV are taken from the Holy Bible, New International Version®, NIV®. Copyright © 1973, 1978, 1984, 2011 by Biblica, Inc.™ Used by permission of Zondervan. All rights reserved worldwide. www.zondervan.com. The "NIV" and "New International Version" are trademarks registered in the United States Patent and Trademark Office by Biblica, Inc.™ | Scripture quotations marked NKJV are taken from the New King James Version®. Copyright © 1982 by Thomas Nelson. Used by permission. All rights reserved. | Scripture quotations marked NLT are taken from the Holy Bible, New Living Translation, copyright © 1996, 2004, 2015 by Tyndale House Foundation. Used by permission of Tyndale House Publishers, Inc., Carol Stream, Illinois 60188. All rights reserved. | Scripture quotations marked ESV are from The ESV® Bible (The Holy Bible, English Standard Version®), copyright © 2001 by Crossway, a publishing ministry of Good News Publishers. Used by permission. All rights reserved. | Scripture quotations marked NASB have been taken from the (NASB®) New American Standard Bible®, Copyright © 2020 by The Lockman Foundation. Used by permission. All rights reserved. www.lockman.org | Scripture quotations marked AMP are taken from the Amplified® Bible (AMP), Copyright © 2015 by The Lockman Foundation. Used by permission. www.lockman.org.

For foreign and subsidiary rights, contact the author.

Cover design by Sara Young

Cover Photo by Andrew van Tilborgh

ISBN: 978-1-954089-91-4   1 2 3 4 5 6 7 8 9 10

Printed in the United States of America

VAN MOODY

GET CLOSER

A
DEVOTIONAL
FOR
ENCOUNTERING
GOD

KUDU

Come close to God, and God will come close to you.

James 4:8a (NLT)

CONTENTS

Introduction 11

Pray First Guide 13

The SOAP Devotional Process 33

SOAP Scripture Reading Plan 35

WEEK 1. FAITH: A Single Sacrifice 49
WEEK 2. FAMILY: Mentoring Others 51
WEEK 3. FINANCES: All She Had 53
WEEK 4. FITNESS: Body and Spirit 55
WEEK 5. FUN: Mandatory Fun! 57

WEEK 6. FAITH: A Roman's Faith 59
WEEK 7. FAMILY: Adopting a Spirit of Honor 61
WEEK 8. FINANCES: Faithful Stewardship 63
WEEK 9. FITNESS: Bought with a Price 65
WEEK 10. FUN: Even More Undignified 67

WEEK 11. FAITH: The Waiting Game 69
WEEK 12. FAMILY: Kids Today 71
WEEK 13. FINANCES: More Than a Mortgage 73
WEEK 14. FITNESS: Still Kicking 75
WEEK 15. FUN: A Festive Faith 77

WEEK 16. FAITH: A Sympathetic High Priest 79
WEEK 17. FAMILY: Father Daughter Problems 81
WEEK 18. FINANCES: Finding Satisfaction 83
WEEK 19. FITNESS: Curbing Our Appetites 85
WEEK 20. FUN: A Joyful Gift 87

WEEK 21. FAITH: Costly Obedience 89
WEEK 22. FAMILY: A Selfless Loyalty 91
WEEK 23. FINANCES: Providing for Your Own 93
WEEK 24. FITNESS: My Strength and My Song 95
WEEK 25. FUN: To Find Satisfaction 97

WEEK 26. FAITH: No Ulterior Motives 99
WEEK 27. FAMILY: A New Family 101
WEEK 28. FINANCES: The Love of Money 103
WEEK 29. FITNESS: A Great Project 105
WEEK 30. FUN: An Eternity of Delight 107

WEEK 31. FAITH: Clinging to the Lord 109
WEEK 32. FAMILY: A New Family Dynamic 111
WEEK 33. FINANCES: Investing in the Future 113
WEEK 34. FITNESS: Run and Not Grow Weary 115
WEEK 35. FUN: A Cheerful Heart 117

WEEK 36. FAITH: Waiting on God 119
WEEK 37. FAMILY: Family Feud 121
WEEK 38. FINANCES: A Den of Robbers 123
WEEK 39. FITNESS: Running with Endurance 125
WEEK 40. FUN: Unshakeable Joy 127

WEEK 41. FAITH: A Gracious and Compassionate God 129
WEEK 42. FAMILY: Sibling Loyalty 131
WEEK 43. FINANCES: Blood Money 133
WEEK 44. FITNESS: Going Against The Grain 135
WEEK 45. FUN: Mandatory R&R 137

WEEK 46. FAITH: The Original 300 139
WEEK 47. FAMILY: Radical Forgiveness 141
WEEK 48. FINANCES: Non-Money Gifts 143
WEEK 49. FITNESS: The Lamp of the Body 145
WEEK 50. FUN: A Little Too Much Fun 147

WEEK 51. FAITH: Choose This Day 149
WEEK 52. FAMILY: A Heavenly Family 151

INTRODUCTION

What does it mean to get closer to God?

If you have believed in Jesus Christ and if He is your Lord and Savior, you're already as close to Jesus—spiritually speaking—as you can get. But this is only the beginning of a person's walk with the Lord. Each day, we have the privilege, the joy, of drawing near to Him. These moments of communion can happen anywhere—in the car, on a run, during the kids' bedtime—but some of the richest moments with God happen when we take time to be alone with Him.

This devotional is designed to make this one-on-one time with Jesus a rhythm in your life. Each week, you'll have a themed devotional to consider, along with practical application questions. As you come back to the topic each day—or several times a week—the Holy Spirit will reveal new truths and realities to you. You'll learn, through Scripture reading and prayer, to more clearly hear the voice of God as He's speaking to you through the Holy Spirit. What greater reward for your time could there be?

There are five main topics spanning fifty-two weeks of study: **faith, family, finances, fitness, and fun**.

FAITH entries take you through scriptural examples of strong faith, showing you that, ultimately, God is the One who nurtures and grows our faith in Him!

FAMILY entries encourage you to reevaluate the health and closeness of your loved ones, no matter what your family "unit" may look like. There's always potential to grow dearer to each other and to become more like Christ in our closest relationships.

FINANCE entries challenge you to consider every aspect of your giving—not just monetary—and check your heart's condition when it comes to surrendering what you have back to the Lord.

FITNESS entries examine your overall health—mental, physical, emotional, and spiritual. We are multifaceted beings, and we were created to be healthy in every area of life. Simple steps can lead to a healthier life right now, today!

FUN entries remind you that recreation, relaxation, and rejuvenation are rhythms that even Jesus embraced during His time on earth. Enjoy a new perspective on "downtime"—it's a spiritual discipline all its own.

In addition, we've included a special section in the beginning of this book called the **Pray First Guide**. This is specifically designed to equip you with practical how-tos of prayer so that you have the knowledge you need to pray at any time, in any situation. You'll learn about different kinds of prayers, along with Scripture references that show examples of those prayers being used; you'll gain key insights on how to connect with God and grow in your faith. All of this is straight from God's Word, and you'll be amazed at how your intimacy with the Lord will grow when you base your prayer life off of the truth of the Bible!

Our prayer is that, over the course of the next fifty-two weeks, you grow in intimacy and faith with the Lord Jesus. In all areas of life, He wants to be your Lord even more prominently than He is today. This is a journey that, while challenging, is eternally rewarding. So set aside time regularly to get closer with your Savior. There's truly no greater calling this side of heaven!

PRAY FIRST GUIDE

ONE OF THE reasons we always begin our year with 21 Days of Fasting and Prayer is because before we do anything else, we should "Pray First". In every situation, whether good or bad, we should always pray before we act. Many times people act first and then want God to bail them out of that situation, but prayer should be our first response, not our last resort.

Understanding the necessity of prayer is not enough. In order for it to become a part of our life, it needs to become something we look forward to doing. I'm convinced most people don't enjoy prayer because they have never been taught how to pray. That's where this simple prayer journal can help. Using several prayer models out of the Bible and having some guides to make prayer more personal, this book is designed to bring joy into your time with God. When you discover the beauty of daily conversation with Him, you'll experience the presence of God that will change your life.

Once you learn how to pray, prayer can become a part of everyday life. And then . . .

Before the day begins—

Before you go to bed—

Before you go to work or school—

Before you send that text—

Before you eat, drive or travel—

When bad things happen—

Before bad things happen—

In every situation—PRAY FIRST!

Prayer changes everything!

LIFESTYLE PRAYER

How do we make prayer a part of our everyday life? We can learn from three things that Jesus did . . .

Very early in the morning, while it was still dark, Jesus got up, left the house and went off to a solitary place, where he prayed.

—MARK 1:35

A CERTAIN TIME

Jesus got up very early in the morning to spend time with His Heavenly Father. In order for prayer to work, we should do the same. Make a daily appointment with God and keep it.

A CERTAIN PLACE

Jesus had a prayer place. Your prayer place needs to be an undistracted environment where you can pray out loud and perhaps have some worship music playing in the background.

A CERTAIN PLAN

Go into your prayer time with a plan. If it changes that's fine. When Jesus taught His disciples how to pray, He gave His disciples a prayer outline. We call it the Lord's Prayer. This outline along with several other tools are available in this book.

THE LORD'S PRAYER

One day Jesus was praying in a certain place. When He finished, one of his disciples said to him, "Lord, teach us to pray . . .".

—LUKE 11:1

"Our Father in heaven, hallowed be your name, your kingdom come, your will be done on earth as it is in heaven. Give us today our daily bread. Forgive us our debts, as we also have forgiven our debtors. And lead us not into temptation, but deliver us from the evil one, for yours is the kingdom and the power and the glory forever."

—MATTHEW 6:9-13

"OUR FATHER IN HEAVEN . . ."

1) CONNECT WITH GOD RELATIONALLY

You have not received a spirit that makes you fearful slaves. Instead, you received God's Spirit when he adopted you as his own children. Now we call him, "Abba, Father."

—ROMANS 8:15 NLT

God loves for us to call Him our Father. Establish your intimate relationship with Him and thank Him for the relationship you have with Him.

". . . HALLOWED BE YOUR NAME . . ."

2) WORSHIP HIS NAME

> *God's name is a place of protection—the righteous can run there and be safe.*
> —PROVERBS 18:10 MSG

What are His Names?

- **Righteousness** – He makes me clean.
- **Sanctifier** – He has called me and set me apart
- **Healer** – He heals all my diseases.
- **Banner of Victory** – He has defeated my enemy.
- **Shepherd** – He speaks to me and leads me.
- **Peace** – He is my peace in every storm.
- **Provider** – He supplies all of my needs

". . . YOUR KINGDOM COME, YOUR WILL BE DONE ON EARTH AS IT IS IN HEAVEN . . ."

3) PRAY HIS AGENDA FIRST

> *He will always give you all you need from day to day if you will make the Kingdom of God your primary concern.*
> —LUKE 12:31 TLB

God's priorities:

- Saving the Lost
- Guiding those in authority – parental, spiritual, governmental, workplace
- His will in us

". . . GIVE US THIS DAY OUR DAILY BREAD . . ."
4) DEPEND ON HIM FOR EVERYTHING

I look up to the mountains—does my help come from there? My help comes from the Lord, who made heaven and earth!
— PSALM 121:1-2 NLT

Ask God for what you want and need and then trust Him for the answer.

". . . FORGIVE US OUR DEBTS AS WE FORGIVE OUR DEBTORS . . ."
5) GET YOUR HEART RIGHT WITH GOD AND PEOPLE

If we confess our sins, he is faithful and just and will forgive us our sins and purify us from all unrighteousness.
— 1 JOHN 1:9

Ask God to check your heart and motives. Receive His forgiveness for any area that He brings to mind. Forgive anyone who has offended you in any way. You can even forgive people in advance.

". . . AND DO NOT LEAD US INTO TEMPTATION BUT DELIVER US FROM THE EVIL ONE . . ."
6) ENGAGE IN SPIRITUAL WARFARE

For our struggle is not against flesh and blood, but against the rulers, against the authorities, against the powers of this dark world and against the spiritual forces of evil in the heavenly realms.
— EPHESIANS 6:12

Take your stand against the enemy and fight the good fight of faith. Every lie that the enemy has told you should be replaced with the truth of God's Word.

"... FOR YOURS IS THE KINGDOM AND THE POWER AND THE GLORY FOREVER."

7) EXPRESS FAITH IN GOD'S ABILITY

> *"Ah, Sovereign LORD, you have made the heavens and the earth by your great power and outstretched arm. Nothing is too hard for you."*
>
> —JEREMIAH 32:17

End your prayer time by reminding yourself of God's ability. Return to praise and make your faith declarations.

"Yours is the Kingdom" – all rule belongs to You.

"Yours is the Power" – all mightiness flows from You.

"Yours is the Glory" – Your victory shall be complete.

TABERNACLE PRAYER

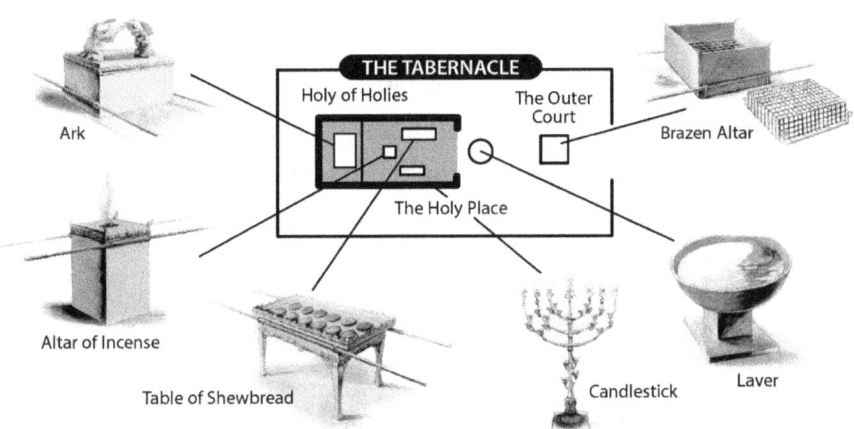

The Tabernacle was the dwelling place of God where He met His people. As they entered the Tabernacle, they passed through seven stations as a protocol to God's presence. Today, these same steps can help us to connect with God and lead us through important elements of prayer.

1) THE OUTER COURT – THANKSGIVING AND PRAISE

Enter his gates with thanksgiving and his courts with praise; give thanks to him and praise his name.

—PSALM 100:4

As the people of God entered the Tabernacle, they came in with thanksgiving on their lips. Thanking God for all the blessings in your life is a great way to begin. Every day, think of a fresh reason why you love and appreciate God.

2) THE BRAZEN ALTAR – THE CROSS OF JESUS

Praise the LORD, my soul, and forget not all his benefits— who forgives all your sins and heals all your diseases, who redeems your life from the pit and crowns you with love and compassion, who satisfies your desires with good things so that your youth is renewed like the eagle's.

—PSALM 103:2-5

In the Old Testament, everyone who had committed sin had to bring animal sacrifices. Jesus paid for all your sins once and for all. You simply need to receive the benefits of what Jesus did for you.

- **Salvation** – God forgives all my sin.
- **Healing** – God heals all my diseases.
- **Redemption** – God rescues me from every attack.
- **Transformation** – God puts His love in me.
- **Provision** – God provides everything I need.

3) THE LAVER – CLEANSING AND PREPARING

Therefore, I urge you, brothers, in view of God's mercy, to offer your bodies as living sacrifices, holy and pleasing to God—this is your spiritual act of worship.

—ROMANS 12:1

The next step in the Tabernacle was a bowl of water where people could wash. Checking your hearts and motives and then surrendering your life to God is an important part of daily prayer. Here are some ways to keep your heart right with God:

- Repent from any known sin.
- Offer your body to God.
- Your tongue – to speak good and not evil
- Your eyes – to see God and the needs of others
- Your ears – to be sensitive to His voice
- Your hands – to do good to others
- Your feet – to walk in God's ways
- Offer your mind to God (Philippians 4:8; Romans 12:2).
- Ask God to give you the fruit of the Spirit (Galatians 5:22-23).

4) THE CANDLESTICK – THE HOLY SPIRIT

The Spirit of the LORD will rest on him—the Spirit of wisdom and of understanding, the Spirit of counsel and of might, the Spirit of the knowledge and fear of the LORD.

—ISAIAH 11:2

The next piece of furniture in the Tabernacle was a seven-branched golden candlestick. The fire represents the Holy Spirit. Every day you should invite the presence of the Holy Spirit into your life.

- The Spirit of the Lord
- The Spirit of Wisdom
- The Spirit of Understanding
- The Spirit of Counsel
- The Spirit of Might
- The Spirit of Knowledge
- The Fear of the Lord

> *You should also ask God to give you spiritual gifts.*
> —1 CORINTHIANS 12:8-10

5) THE TABLE OF SHEWBREAD – THE WORD OF GOD

> *Keep this Book of the Law always on your lips; meditate on it day and night, so that you may be careful to do everything written in it. Then you will be prosperous and successful.*
> —JOSHUA 1:8

A table with twelve loaves of bread represents the importance of reading God's Word for daily sustenance. With this in mind, here are ways to nourish your soul:

- Read God's Word.
- Claim His many great promises.
- Ask for fresh revelation of the Word.
- Take time to read and meditate on the Word.
- Get a Word for the day.

6) THE ALTAR OF INCENSE – WORSHIP

> *The name of the LORD is a strong tower; the righteous run to it and are safe.*
> —PROVERBS 18:10

A small altar of burning incense stood at the entrance to the Holy of Holies, where God's presence dwelt. This altar represents worship. The people of God literally entered God's presence worshipping the Names of God, including:

- God is My Righteousness – Jeremiah 23:6
- God is My Sanctifier – Leviticus 20:7-8
- God is My Healer – Exodus 15:26
- God is My Provider – Genesis 22:14
- God is My Banner of Victory – Exodus 17:15
- God is My Peace – Judges 6:24
- God is My Shepherd – Psalm 23:1
- God is Always There – Ezekiel 48:35

7) THE ARK OF THE COVENANT – INTERCESSION

I urge, then, first of all, that requests, prayers, intercession and thanksgiving be made for everyone—for kings and all those in authority, that we may live peaceful and quiet lives in all godliness and holiness. This is good, and pleases God our Savior, who wants all men to be saved and to come to a knowledge of the truth.

—1 TIMOTHY 2:1-4

The final place in the Tabernacle was the place where God's presence dwelt. It was there that the priest interceded on behalf of the people. In the New Testament, you and I are all called priests and instructed to intercede for others.

- Those in authority – spiritual, civil, family, and workplace
- My family
- My church – pastor, small group, members, and vision/mission
- My city, nation, and world
- My needs

PRAYER AND SCRIPTURE DEVOTIONAL

This is a great prayer outline mixed with Scripture readings. Simply walk through the outline while you look up the passages of Scripture.

1) **THANKSGIVING AND PRAISE – PRESENT YOURSELF TO GOD (MARK 12:30)**

Think of a fresh reason to thank Him (Psalm 100:4, 118:24). Present your body in worship (Romans 12:1; Psalm 63-3,4) by:

- Kneeling before Him as your Lord
- Lifting your hands to Him as your Source
- Standing in praise before Him as your King
- Clapping your hands with rejoicing
- Dancing with joy as a child
- Bowing your head in humility

Sing a new song to Him (Psalm 96:1,2; Colossians 3:16).

Invite Holy-Spirit-assisted praise (Jude 20; 1 Corinthians 14:15).

2) **CONFESSION AND CLEANSING – PRESENT YOUR HEART TO GOD (PROVERBS 4:23)**

Ask God to search your heart (Psalm 139:23, 24) for:

- Sin – receive cleansing and righteousness
- Selfishness – receive holiness and sanctification
- Stress – receive life and power
- Sickness – receive healing and strength

Remember the danger of self-deception (Jeremiah 17:9; 1 John 1:6-10).

Set a monitor on your mouth and heart (Psalm 19:14, 49:3).

Ask God to help you keep His purposes and goals in view (Psalm 90:12; Philippians 3:13-14).

3) ORDER AND OBEDIENCE – PRESENT YOUR DAY TO GOD (PSALM 37:5)

Present the day's details (Psalm 37:4,5, 31:14,15; Deuteronomy 33:25):

- Choose the fear of the Lord.
- Commit your works to God.

Indicate your dependence upon God (Proverbs 3:5-7; Psalm 131:1-3).

Request specific direction for actions and decisions (Psalm 25:4,5; Isaiah 30:21).

Choose to obey God's explicit instructions (Matthew 6:11, 7:7-8).

- In the Word of God
- By choosing to do His will

WARFARE PRAYERS

Prayer is not only communion with God; it is confrontation with the enemy. These prayers are very helpful in spiritual warfare.

> *Put on the full armor of God so that you can take your stand against the devil's schemes. For our struggle is not against flesh and blood, but against the rulers, against the authorities, against the powers of this dark world and against the spiritual forces of evil in the heavenly realms. Therefore put on the full armor of God, so that when the day of evil comes, you may be able to stand your ground, and after you have done everything, to stand. Stand firm then with the belt of truth buckled around your waist, with the breastplate of righteousness in place, and with your feet fitted with the readiness that comes from the Gospel of peace. In addition to all this, take up the shield of faith, with which you can extinguish all the flaming arrows of the evil one. Take the helmet of salvation and the sword of the Spirit, which is the Word of God. And pray in the Spirit on all occasions*

with all kinds of prayers and requests. With this in mind, be alert and always keep on praying for all the Lord's people.
—EPHESIANS 6:11-18

THE ARMOR OF GOD

(based on Ephesians 6:13-17)

"Thank You, Lord, for my salvation. I receive it in a new and fresh way from You and I declare that nothing can separate me from the love of Christ and the place I have in Your kingdom. I wear Your righteousness today against all condemnation and corruption. Cover me with Your holiness and purity—defend me from all assaults against my heart.

Lord, I put on the belt of truth. I choose a lifestyle of honesty and integrity. Expose the lies I have believed, and show me the truths I need today. I choose to live for the Gospel in every moment. Show me where You are working and lead me to it. Give me strength to walk daily with You. I believe that You are powerful against every lie and assault of the enemy. You have good in store for me. Nothing is coming today that can overcome me because You are with me. Holy Spirit, show me the truths of the Word of God that I will need to counter the traps of the enemy. Bring those Scriptures to mind today.

Finally, Holy Spirit, I agree to walk in step with You in everything as my spirit communes with You in prayer throughout the day."

THE WEAPONS OF WARFARE

(based on 2 Corinthians 10:4-5)

"Father, Your Word says that no weapon formed against me shall prosper (Isaiah 54:17). Therefore I declare that no weapon formed against me prospers this day or any day to come in Jesus' name. Your Word says that trouble will not arise a second time (Nahum 1:9). Therefore I declare that Satan cannot make trouble for me again, in this manner, as he did in the past in Jesus' name. I declare all of these prayers accomplished and brought to pass by trusting you through faith and expectation in the name of Jesus.

Lord Jesus, I confess to You all of my sins this day, yesterday and every day past. I repent and renounce them, those known and unknown, those of omission and commission, in what I have done and in what I have failed to do. I lay down at Your feet all of the sins of the flesh, the tongue, and of the heart, and all unholy thoughts and actions. Thank You, Lord, for shedding Your precious blood for me.

I stand on Your Word. The enemy is driven out from before me, above me, around me, and below me; from my home, workplace, church and its ministries, children, and loved ones; from my works and labors, land, and my presence. I declare that he is not able to stand against me, and his works are taken captive and destroyed. No weapon formed against me will prosper, for the Spirit of the Lord shall raise a standard against them. I declare all of these things accomplished by Your Word. Jesus, my Lord, I give You thanksgiving, praise, glory, honor and worship for Your righteousness and holiness given to me by Your Word on my behalf."

PROTECTION PRAYER

(based on 2 Corinthians 6:14—7:1, 10:3-5; Romans 12:1, 2)

"Heavenly Father, I bow in worship and praise before You. I cover myself with the blood of the Lord Jesus Christ as my protection. I surrender myself completely and unreservedly in every area of my life to You. I submit myself only to the true and living God and refuse any involvement of the enemy in my life. I choose to be transformed by the renewing of my mind. I pull down every thought that exalts itself against the knowledge of Christ. I pray and thank you for a sound mind, the mind of Christ.

Today and every day I ask for protection over my spouse; each of my children; our immediate family members, relatives, friends, acquaintances and myself. I also ask today for protection during all of our travels; for our provision, finances, possessions, health, safety, and welfare. I put all of these things under the covering of Your precious blood and declare that Satan cannot touch them, on this day or any day to come."

GENERAL CONFESSION PRAYER

(based on Romans 10:10; James 5:16; I John 1:7-9, 3:8)

"Lord Jesus, I believe that You are the Son of God. You are the Messiah, come in the flesh to destroy the works of the devil. You died on the cross for my sins and rose again the third day from the dead. I now confess all my sins and repent. I receive your forgiveness and ask you to cleanse me from all sin. Thank You for redeeming me, cleansing me, justifying me, and sanctifying me in Your blood."

FORGIVENESS PRAYER

(based on Matthew 6:14,15; Leviticus 19:18)

"Lord, I have a confession to make. I have not loved, but have resented certain people and have unforgiveness in my heart. I call upon You, Lord, to help me forgive them. I do now forgive (name them). I also forgive and accept myself in the name of Jesus Christ."

PRIDE PRAYER

(based on Proverbs 11:2, 16:18, 26:12; 1 Timothy 3:6)

"Father, I come to You in the name of the Lord Jesus Christ. I know pride is an abomination to You. I renounce anything that would cause me to have pride in my heart in dealing with other people. I renounce these and turn away from them. I humble myself before You and come to You as a little child."

Study Proverbs 6:16-19 and remember that fasting is a means by which a person humbles himself before the Lord.

GENERATIONAL BONDAGE PRAYER

(based on Exodus 20:4-6, 34:7; Numbers 14:18)

"In the name of the Lord Jesus Christ, I now renounce, break, and loose myself from all bondages or bonds of physical or mental illness upon me, my family or family line as the result of parents or any other ancestors. I thank You, Lord, for setting me free."

PERSONAL PRAYER TARGETS

I urge, then, first of all, that requests, prayers, intercession and thanksgiving be made for everyone—for kings and all those in authority, that we may live peaceful and quiet lives in all godliness and holiness. This is good, and pleases God our Savior, who wants all men to be saved and to come to a knowledge of the truth.

—1 TIMOTHY 2:1-4

Pray for those in authority and those under your authority.

MY GOVERNMENT

President _____

National leaders _____

State leaders _____

_____

City leaders _____

_____

MY FAMILY

Spouse _____

Children _____

_____

Parents _____

Siblings _____

_____

Extended family _____

_____

_____

MY CHURCH

Pastor _____

Small group leader _____

Small group members _____

_____

_____

MY LIFE

Employer _____

Co-workers _____

_____

_____

Employees _____

_____

_____

Teachers/Professors _____

_____

THOSE I INFLUENCE

Close friends _____

_____
_____
_____
_____
_____
_____

THOSE WHO NEED GOD

_____
_____
_____
_____
_____
_____
_____
_____
_____
_____

1) PRAY THAT THE FATHER WOULD DRAW THEM TO JESUS

> *No one can come to me unless the Father*
> *who sent me draws him.*
>
> —JOHN 6:44

2) BIND THE SPIRIT THAT BLINDS THEIR MINDS

> *The god of this age has blinded the minds of unbelievers,*
> *so that they cannot see the light of the gospel of*
> *the glory of Christ, who is the image of God.*
>
> —2 CORINTHIANS 4:4

3) LOOSE THE SPIRIT OF ADOPTION (SONSHIP)

> *For you did not receive a spirit that makes you a*
> *slave again to fear; but you received the Spirit of*
> *sonship. And by him we cry, "Abba, Father."*
>
> —ROMANS 8:15

4) PRAY THAT OTHER BELIEVERS WILL CROSS THEIR PATHS AND ENTER INTO POSITIVE RELATIONSHIPS WITH THEM

> *Ask the Lord of the harvest, therefore, to send*
> *out workers into his harvest field.*
>
> —MATTHEW 9:38

5) LOOSE THE SPIRIT OF WISDOM AND REVELATION ON THEM SO THEY MAY KNOW GOD BETTER

> *I keep asking that the God of our Lord Jesus Christ,*
> *the glorious Father, may give you the Spirit of wisdom*
> *and revelation, so that you may know him better.*
>
> —EPHESIANS 1:17

THE SOAP DEVOTIONAL PROCESS

S.O.A.P. is the devotional method that I have practiced for years, and it's the devotional method I lay out in this journal. The acronym **S.O.A.P.** stands for Scripture, Observation, Application, and Prayer. It is a great way of getting more out of your time with God and in His Word. Just like physical soap, this devotional method will wash you spiritually, transform your heart and bring you closer to God than ever before. I did not invent this method; rather, it was taught to me by a mentor, and I am honored to share it with you through this journal.

In order to do this daily, you only need four things:

1. A Time

Set an appointment with God and keep it every day.

2. A Place

Find a great place. It can be your kitchen or a coffee shop. Any place that's comfortable and quiet for you works.

3. A Bible

Get a version that is easy to read and understand. My favorite versions of the Bible are the NIV, Message, NLT, NKJV, TLB and Amplified.

4. A Journal

What you hold in your hand is a great journal designed for you to write in. The Bible Reading Plan to do your S.O.A.P. Devotion is on the following pages.

In your journal, focus on 4 distinct areas:

Scripture

Each day, as you do your daily Bible reading, there will be a verse or a few verses that will grab your heart. Write the verse or verses that spoke to you during your reading.

Observation

Write down what the context of the Scripture is. What is happening? Who is it happening to? Why is it happening? This is just your general observation of what is taking place in the verse or verses.

Application

How does the Scripture apply to what is happening to you or in your environment currently? This is where you write down what the verse or verses mean to you, what you hear God saying to you through the Scriptures.

Prayer

Write a prayer to God based on what you just learned and ask Him to help you apply this truth in your life.

Following this devotional method daily will radically touch your heart and bring you closer to God than ever before.

SOAP SCRIPTURE READING PLAN

Following this devotional method daily will radically touch your heart and bring you closer to God than ever before.

- ❏ January 1 . . . . Genesis 1–2; Luke 1
- ❏ January 2 . . . . Genesis 3–5; Luke 2
- ❏ January 3 . . . . Genesis 6–8; Luke 3
- ❏ January 4 . . . . Genesis 9–11; Luke 4
- ❏ January 5 . . . . Genesis 12–14; Luke 5
- ❏ January 6 . . . . Genesis 15–17; Luke 6
- ❏ January 7 . . . . Genesis 18–19; Psalm 3; Luke 7
- ❏ January 8 . . . . Genesis 20–22; Luke 8
- ❏ January 9 . . . . Genesis 23–24; Luke 9
- ❏ January 10 . . . . Genesis 25–26; Psalm 6; Luke 10
- ❏ January 11 . . . . Genesis 27–28; Psalm 4; Luke 11
- ❏ January 12 . . . . Genesis 29–30; Luke 12
- ❏ January 13 . . . . Genesis 31–33; Luke 13
- ❏ January 14 . . . . Genesis 34–36; Luke 14
- ❏ January 15 . . . . Genesis 37–38; Psalm 7; Luke 15
- ❏ January 16 . . . . Genesis 39–41; Luke 16
- ❏ January 17 . . . . Genesis 42–43; Psalm 5; Luke 17
- ❏ January 18 . . . . Genesis 44–46; Luke 18
- ❏ January 19 . . . . Genesis 47–48; Psalm 10; Luke 19
- ❏ January 20 . . . . Genesis 49–50; Psalm 8; Luke 20
- ❏ January 21 . . . . Exodus 1–2; Psalm 88; Luke 21
- ❏ January 22 . . . . Exodus 3–5; Luke 22
- ❏ January 23 . . . . Exodus 6–8; Luke 23
- ❏ January 24 . . . . Exodus 9–11; Luke 24

DATE	SCRIPTURE READING
☐ January 25	Exodus 12–13; Psalm 21; Acts 1
☐ January 26	Exodus 14–16; Acts 2
☐ January 27	Exodus 17–20; Acts 3
☐ January 28	Exodus 21–22; Psalm 12; Acts 4
☐ January 29	Exodus 23–24; Psalm 14; Acts 5
☐ January 30	Exodus 25–27; Acts 6
☐ January 31	Exodus 28–29; Acts 7
☐ February 1	Exodus 30–32; Acts 8
☐ February 2	Exodus 33–34; Psalm 16; Acts 9
☐ February 3	Exodus 35–36; Acts 10
☐ February 4	Exodus 37–38; Psalm 19; Acts 11
☐ February 5	Exodus 39–40; Psalm 15; Acts 12
☐ February 6	Leviticus 1–3; Acts 13
☐ February 7	Leviticus 4–6; Acts 14
☐ February 8	Leviticus 7–9; Acts 15
☐ February 9	Leviticus 10–12; Acts 16
☐ February 10	Leviticus 13–14; Acts 17
☐ February 11	Leviticus 15–17; Acts 18
☐ February 12	Leviticus 18–19; Psalm 13; Acts 19
☐ February 13	Leviticus 20–22; Acts 20
☐ February 14	Leviticus 23–24; Psalm 24; Acts 21
☐ February 15	Leviticus 25; Psalm 25–26; Acts 22
☐ February 16	Leviticus 26–27; Acts 23
☐ February 17	Numbers 1–2; Acts 24
☐ February 18	Numbers 3–4; Acts 25
☐ February 19	Numbers 5–6; Psalm 22; Acts 26
☐ February 20	Numbers 7; Psalm 23; Acts 27
☐ February 21	Numbers 8–9; Acts 28
☐ February 22	Numbers 10–11; Psalm 27; Mark 1
☐ February 23	Numbers 12–13; Psalm 90; Mark 2
☐ February 24	Numbers 14–16; Mark 3
☐ February 25	Numbers 17–18; Psalm 29; Mark 4
☐ February 26	Numbers 19–20; Psalm 28; Mark 5

SOAP SCRIPTURE READING PLAN

DATE   SCRIPTURE READING

- February 27 .... Numbers 21–23; Mark 6–7
- February 28 .... Numbers 24–27; 1 Corinthians 13
- March 1 .... Numbers 28–29; Mark 8
- March 2 .... Numbers 30–31; Mark 9
- March 3 .... Numbers 32–33; Mark 10
- March 4 .... Numbers 34–36; Mark 11
- March 5 .... Deuteronomy 1–2; Mark 12
- March 6 .... Deuteronomy 3–4; Psalm 36; Mark 13
- March 7 .... Deuteronomy 5–6; Psalm 43; Mark 14
- March 8 .... Deuteronomy 7–9; Mark 15
- March 9 .... Deuteronomy 10–12; Mark 16
- March 10 .... Deuteronomy 13–15; Galatians 1
- March 11 .... Deuteronomy 16–18; Psalm 38; Galatians 2
- March 12 .... Deuteronomy 19–21; Galatians 3
- March 13 .... Deuteronomy 22–24; Galatians 4
- March 14 .... Deuteronomy 25–27; Galatians 5
- March 15 .... Deuteronomy 28–29; Galatians 6
- March 16 .... Deuteronomy 30–31; Psalm 40; 1 Corinthians 1
- March 17 .... Deuteronomy 32–34; 1 Corinthians 2
- March 18 .... Joshua 1–2; Psalm 37; 1 Corinthians 3
- March 19 .... Joshua 3–6; 1 Corinthians 4
- March 20 .... Joshua 7–8; Psalm 69; 1 Corinthians 5
- March 21 .... Joshua 9–11; 1 Corinthians 6
- March 22 .... Joshua 12–14; 1 Corinthians 7
- March 23 .... Joshua 15–17; 1 Corinthians 8
- March 24 .... Joshua 18–20; 1 Corinthians 9
- March 25 .... Joshua 21–22; Psalm 47; 1 Corinthians 10
- March 26 .... Joshua 23–24; Psalm 44; 1 Corinthians 11
- March 27 .... Judges 1–3; 1 Corinthians 12
- March 28 .... Judges 4–5; Psalm 39, 41; 1 Corinthians 13
- March 29 .... Judges 6–7; Psalm 52; 1 Corinthians 14
- March 30 .... Judges 8; Psalm 42; 1 Corinthians 15
- March 31 .... Judges 9–10; Psalm 49; 1 Corinthians 16

DATE	SCRIPTURE READING
❏ April 1	Judges 11–12; Psalm 50; 2 Corinthians 1
❏ April 2	Judges 13–16; 2 Corinthians 2
❏ April 3	Judges 17–18; Psalm 89; 2 Corinthians 3
❏ April 4	Judges 19–21; 2 Corinthians 4
❏ April 5	Ruth 1–2; Psalm 53, 61; 2 Corinthians 5
❏ April 6	Ruth 3–4; Psalm 64–65; 2 Corinthians 6
❏ April 7	1 Samuel 1–2; Psalm 66; 2 Corinthians 7
❏ April 8	1 Samuel 3–5; Psalm 77; 2 Corinthians 8
❏ April 9	1 Samuel 6–7; Psalm 72; 2 Corinthians 9
❏ April 10	1 Samuel 8–10; 2 Corinthians 10
❏ April 11	1 Samuel 11–12; 1 Chronicles 1; 2 Corinthians 11
❏ April 12	1 Samuel 13; 1 Chronicles 2–3; 2 Corinthians 12
❏ April 13	1 Samuel 14; 1 Chronicles 4; 2 Corinthians 13
❏ April 14	1 Samuel 15–16; 1 Chronicles 5; Matthew 1
❏ April 15	1 Samuel 17; Psalm 9; Matthew 2
❏ April 16	1 Samuel 18; 1 Chronicles 6; Psalm 11; Matthew 3
❏ April 17	1 Samuel 19; 1 Chronicles 7; Psalm 59; Matthew 4
❏ April 18	1 Samuel 20–21; Psalm 34; Matthew 5
❏ April 19	1 Samuel 22; Psalm 17, 35; Matthew 6
❏ April 20	1 Samuel 23; Psalm 31, 54; Matthew 7
❏ April 21	1 Samuel 24; Psalm 57–58; 1 Chronicles 8; Matthew 8
❏ April 22	1 Samuel 25–26; Psalm 63; Matthew 9
❏ April 23	1 Samuel 27; Psalm 141, 1 Chronicles 9; Matthew 10
❏ April 24	1 Samuel 28–29; Psalm 109; Matthew 11
❏ April 25	1 Samuel 30–31; 1 Chronicles 10; Matthew 12
❏ April 26	2 Samuel 1; Psalm 140; Matthew 13
❏ April 27	2 Samuel 2; 1 Chronicles 11; Psalm 142; Matthew 14
❏ April 28	2 Samuel 3; 1 Chronicles 12; Matthew 15
❏ April 29	2 Samuel 4–5; Psalm 139; Matthew 16
❏ April 30	2 Samuel 6; 1 Chronicles 13; Psalm 68; Matthew 17

SOAP SCRIPTURE READING PLAN

DATE   SCRIPTURE READING

- ❏ May 1 . . . . 1 Chronicles 14-15; Psalm 132; Matthew 18
- ❏ May 2 . . . . 1 Chronicles 16; Psalm 106; Matthew 19
- ❏ May 3 . . . . 2 Samuel 7; 1 Chronicles 17; Psalm 2; Matthew 20
- ❏ May 4 . . . . 2 Samuel 8-9; 1 Chronicles 18-19; Matthew 21
- ❏ May 5 . . . . 2 Samuel 10; 1 Chronicles 20; Psalm 20; Matthew 22
- ❏ May 6 . . . . 2 Samuel 11-12; Psalm 51; Matthew 23
- ❏ May 7 . . . . 2 Samuel 13-14; Matthew 24
- ❏ May 8 . . . . 2 Samuel 15-16; Psalm 32; Matthew 25
- ❏ May 9 . . . . 2 Samuel 17; Psalm 71; Matthew 26
- ❏ May 10 . . . . 2 Samuel 18; Psalm 56; Matthew 27
- ❏ May 11 . . . . 2 Samuel 19-20; Psalm 55; Matthew 28
- ❏ May 12 . . . . 2 Samuel 21-23; 1 Thessalonians 1
- ❏ May 13 . . . . 2 Samuel 24; 1 Chronicles 21; Psalm 30; 1 Thessalonians 2
- ❏ May 14 . . . . 1 Chronicles 22-24; 1 Thessalonians 3
- ❏ May 15 . . . . 1 Chronicles 25-27; 1 Thessalonians 4
- ❏ May 16 . . . . 1 Kings 1; 1 Chronicles 28; Psalm 91; 1 Thessalonians 5
- ❏ May 17 . . . . 1 Kings 2; 1 Chronicles 29; Psalm 95; 2 Thessalonians 1
- ❏ May 18 . . . . 1 Kings 3; 2 Chronicles 1; Psalm 78; 2 Thessalonians 2
- ❏ May 19 . . . . 1 Kings 4-5; 2 Chronicles 2; Psalm 101; 2 Thessalonians 3
- ❏ May 20 . . . . 1 Kings 6; 2 Chronicles 3; Psalm 97; Romans 1
- ❏ May 21 . . . . 1 Kings 7; 2 Chronicles 4; Psalm 98; Romans 2
- ❏ May 22 . . . . 1 Kings 8; 2 Chronicles 5; Psalm 99; Romans 3
- ❏ May 23 . . . . 2 Chronicles 6-7; Psalm 135; Romans 4
- ❏ May 24 . . . . 1 Kings 9; 2 Chronicles 8; Psalm 136; Romans 5
- ❏ May 25 . . . . 1 Kings 10-11; 2 Chronicles 9; Romans 6
- ❏ May 26 . . . . Proverbs 1-3; Romans 7
- ❏ May 27 . . . . Proverbs 4-6; Romans 8

DATE	SCRIPTURE READING
❏ May 28	Proverbs 7-9; Romans 9
❏ May 29	Proverbs 10-12; Romans 10
❏ May 30	Proverbs 13-15; Romans 11
❏ May 31	Proverbs 16-18; Romans 12
❏ June 1	Proverbs 19-21; Romans 13
❏ June 2	Proverbs 22-24; Romans 14
❏ June 3	Proverbs 25-27; Romans 15
❏ June 4	Proverbs 28-29; Psalm 60; Romans 16
❏ June 5	Proverbs 30-31; Psalm 33; Ephesians 1
❏ June 6	Ecclesiastes 1-3; Psalm 45; Ephesians 2
❏ June 7	Ecclesiastes 4-6; Psalm 18; Ephesians 3
❏ June 8	Ecclesiastes 7-9; Ephesians 4
❏ June 9	Ecclesiastes 10-12; Psalm 94; Ephesians 5
❏ June 10	Song of Songs 1-4; Ephesians 6
❏ June 11	Song of Songs 5-8; Philippians 1
❏ June 12	1 Kings 12; 2 Chronicles 10-11; Philippians 2
❏ June 13	1 Kings 13-14; 2 Chronicles 12; Philippians 3
❏ June 14	1 Kings 15; 2 Chronicles; 13-14; Philippians 4
❏ June 15	1 Kings 16; 2 Chronicles 15-16; Colossians 1
❏ June 16	1 Kings 17-19; Colossians 2
❏ June 17	1 Kings 20-21; 2 Chronicles 17; Colossians 3
❏ June 18	1 Kings 22; 2 Chronicles 18-19; Colossians 4
❏ June 19	2 Kings 1-3; Psalm 82; 1 Timothy 1
❏ June 20	2 Kings 4-5; Psalm 83; 1 Timothy 2
❏ June 21	2 Kings 6-7; 2 Chronicles 20; 1 Timothy 3
❏ June 22	2 Kings 8-9; 2 Chronicles 21; 1 Timothy 4
❏ June 23	2 Kings 10; 2 Chronicles 22-23; 1 Timothy 5
❏ June 24	2 Kings 11-12; 2 Chronicles 24; 1 Timothy 6
❏ June 25	Joel 1-3; 2 Timothy 1
❏ June 26	Jonah 1-4; 2 Timothy 2
❏ June 27	2 Kings 13-14; 2 Chronicles 25; 2 Timothy 3
❏ June 28	Amos 1-3; Psalm 80; 2 Timothy 4
❏ June 29	Amos 4-6; Psalm 86; Titus 1

SOAP SCRIPTURE READING PLAN

DATE	SCRIPTURE READING
☐ June 30	Amos 7–9; Psalm 104; Titus 2
☐ July 1	Isaiah 1–3; Titus 3
☐ July 2	Isaiah 4–5; Psalm 115–116; Jude
☐ July 3	Isaiah 6–7; 2 Chronicles 26–27; Philemon
☐ July 4	2 Kings 15–16; Hosea 1; Hebrews 1
☐ July 5	Hosea 2–5; Hebrews 2
☐ July 6	Hosea 6–9; Hebrews 3
☐ July 7	Hosea 10–12; Psalm 73; Hebrews 4
☐ July 8	Hosea 13–14; Psalm 100, 102; Hebrews 5
☐ July 9	Micah 1–4; Hebrews 6
☐ July 10	Micah 5–7; Hebrews 7
☐ July 11	Isaiah 8–10; Hebrews 8
☐ July 12	Isaiah 11–14; Hebrews 9
☐ July 13	Isaiah 15–18; Hebrews 10
☐ July 14	Isaiah 19–21; Hebrews 11
☐ July 15	Isaiah 22–24; Hebrews 12
☐ July 16	Isaiah 25–28; Hebrews 13
☐ July 17	Isaiah 29–31; James 1
☐ July 18	Isaiah 32–35; James 2
☐ July 19	2 Kings 17; 2 Chronicles 28; Psalm 46; James 3
☐ July 20	2 Chronicles 29–31; James 4
☐ July 21	2 Kings 18–19; 2 Chronicles 32; James 5
☐ July 22	Isaiah 36–37; Psalm 76; 1 Peter 1
☐ July 23	2 Kings 20; Isaiah 38–39; Psalm 75; 1 Peter 2
☐ July 24	Isaiah 40–42; 1 Peter 3
☐ July 25	Isaiah 43–45; 1 Peter 4
☐ July 26	Isaiah 46–49; 1 Peter 5
☐ July 27	Isaiah 50–52; Psalm 92; 2 Peter 1
☐ July 28	Isaiah 53–56; 2 Peter 2
☐ July 29	Isaiah 57–59; Psalm 103; 2 Peter 3
☐ July 30	Isaiah 60–62; John 1
☐ July 31	Isaiah 63–64; Psalm 107; John 2
☐ August 1	Isaiah 65–66; Psalm 62; John 3

DATE	**SCRIPTURE READING**
❏ August 2	2 Kings 21; 2 Chronicles 33; John 4
❏ August 3	Nahum 1–3; John 5
❏ August 4	2 Kings 22; 2 Chronicles 34; John 6
❏ August 5	2 Kings 23; 2 Chronicles 35; John 7
❏ August 6	Habakkuk; 1–3; John 8
❏ August 7	Zephaniah 1–3; John 9
❏ August 8	Jeremiah 1–2; John 10
❏ August 9	Jeremiah 3–4; John 11
❏ August 10	Jeremiah 5–6; John 12
❏ August 11	Jeremiah 7–9; John 13
❏ August 12	Jeremiah 10–12; John 14
❏ August 13	Jeremiah 13–15; John 15
❏ August 14	Jeremiah 16–17; Psalm 96; John 16
❏ August 15	Jeremiah 18–20; Psalm 93; John 17
❏ August 16	Kings 24; Jeremiah 22; Psalm 112; John 18
❏ August 17	Jeremiah 23, 25; John 19
❏ August 18	Jeremiah 26, 35, 36; John 20
❏ August 19	Jeremiah 45–47; Psalm 105; John 21
❏ August 20	Jeremiah 48–49; Psalm 67; 1 John 1
❏ August 21	Jeremiah 21, 24, 27; Psalm 118; 1 John 2
❏ August 22	Jeremiah 28–30; 1 John 3
❏ August 23	Jeremiah 31–32; 1 John 4
❏ August 24	Jeremiah 33–34; Psalm 74; 1 John 5
❏ August 25	Jeremiah 37–39; Psalm 79; 2 John
❏ August 26	Jeremiah 50–51; 3 John
❏ August 27	Jeremiah 52; Revelation 1; Psalm 143–144
❏ August 28	Ezekiel 1–3; Revelation 2
❏ August 29	Ezekiel 4–7; Revelation 3
❏ August 30	Ezekiel 8–11; Revelation 4
❏ August 31	Ezekiel 12–14; Revelation 5
❏ September 1	Ezekiel 15–16; Psalm 70; Revelation 6
❏ September 2	Ezekiel 17–19; Revelation 7
❏ September 3	Ezekiel 20–21; Psalm 111; Revelation 8

SOAP SCRIPTURE READING PLAN

DATE   **SCRIPTURE READING**

- ☐ September 4 . . . . Ezekiel 22–24; Revelation 9
- ☐ September 5 . . . . Ezekiel 25–28; Revelation 10
- ☐ September 6 . . . . Ezekiel 29–32; Revelation 11
- ☐ September 7 . . . . 2 Kings 25; 2 Chronicles 36; Jeremiah 40–41; Revelation 12
- ☐ September 8 . . . . Jeremiah 42–44; Psalm 48; Revelation 13
- ☐ September 9 . . . . Lamentations 1–2; Obadiah; Revelation 14
- ☐ September 10 . . . . Lamentations 3–5; Revelation 15
- ☐ September 11 . . . . Daniel 1–2; Revelation 16
- ☐ September 12 . . . . Daniel 3–4; Psalm 81; Revelation 17
- ☐ September 13 . . . . Ezekiel 33–35; Revelation 18
- ☐ September 14 . . . . Ezekiel 36–37; Psalm 110; Revelation 19
- ☐ September 15 . . . . Ezekiel 38–39; Psalm 145; Revelation 20
- ☐ September 16 . . . . Ezekiel 40–41; Psalm 128; Revelation 21
- ☐ September 17 . . . . Ezekiel 42–44; Revelation 22
- ☐ September 18 . . . . Ezekiel 45–46; Luke 1
- ☐ September 19 . . . . Ezekiel 47–48; Luke 2
- ☐ September 20 . . . . Daniel 5–6; Psalm 130; Luke 3
- ☐ September 21 . . . . Daniel 7–8; Psalm 137; Luke 4
- ☐ September 22 . . . . Daniel 9–10; Psalm 123; Luke 5
- ☐ September 23 . . . . Daniel 11–12; Luke 6
- ☐ September 24 . . . . Ezra 1; Psalm 84–85; Luke 7
- ☐ September 25 . . . . Ezra 2–3; Luke 8
- ☐ September 26 . . . . Ezra 4; Psalm 113, 127; Luke 9
- ☐ September 27 . . . . Haggai 1–2; Psalm 129; Luke 10
- ☐ September 28 . . . . Zechariah 1–3; Luke 11
- ☐ September 29 . . . . Zechariah 4–6; Luke 12
- ☐ September 30 . . . . Zechariah 7–9; Luke 13
- ☐ October 1 . . . . Zechariah 10–12; Psalm 126; Luke 14
- ☐ October 2 . . . . Zechariah 13–14; Psalm 147; Luke 15
- ☐ October 3 . . . . Ezra 5–6; Psalm 138; Luke 16
- ☐ October 4 . . . . Esther 1–2; Psalm 150; Luke 17
- ☐ October 5 . . . . Esther 3–8; Luke 18

DATE	**SCRIPTURE READING**
❏ October 6	Esther 9–10; Luke 19
❏ October 7	Ezra 7–8; Luke 20
❏ October 8	Ezra 9–10; Psalm 131; Luke 21
❏ October 9	Nehemiah 1–2; Psalm 133; Luke 22
❏ October 10	Nehemiah 3–4; Luke 23
❏ October 11	Nehemiah 5–6; Psalm 146; Luke 24
❏ October 12	Nehemiah 7–8; Acts 1
❏ October 13	Nehemiah 9–10; Acts 2
❏ October 14	Nehemiah 11–12; Psalm 1; Acts 3
❏ October 15	Nehemiah 13; Malachi 1–2; Acts 4
❏ October 16	Malachi 3–4; Psalm 148; Acts 5
❏ October 17	Job 1–2; Acts 6–7
❏ October 18	Job 3; Acts 8–9
❏ October 19	Job 4–5; Psalm 108; Acts 10–11
❏ October 20	Job 6–7; Acts 12
❏ October 21	Job 8; Acts 13–14
❏ October 22	Job 9–10; Acts 15–16
❏ October 23	Job 11; Acts 17–18
❏ October 24	Job 12–14; Acts 19–20
❏ October 25	Job 15; Acts 21–23
❏ October 26	Job 16–17; Acts 24–26
❏ October 27	Job 18; Psalm 114; Acts 27–28
❏ October 28	Job 19; Mark 1–2
❏ October 29	Job 20; Mark 3–4
❏ October 30	Job 21; Mark 5–6
❏ October 31	Job 22; Mark 7–8
❏ November 1	Psalm 121; Mark 9–10
❏ November 2	Job 23–24; Mark 11–12
❏ November 3	Job 25; Mark 13–14
❏ November 4	Job 26–27; Mark 15–16
❏ November 5	Job 28–29; Galatians 1–2
❏ November 6	Job 30; Psalm 120; Galatians 3–4
❏ November 7	Job 31–32; Galatians 5–6

SOAP SCRIPTURE READING PLAN

DATE   SCRIPTURE READING

- ❏ November 8 . . . . Job 33; 1 Corinthians 1-3
- ❏ November 9 . . . . Job 34; 1 Corinthians 4-6
- ❏ November 10 . . . . Job 35-36; 1 Corinthians 7-8
- ❏ November 11 . . . . Psalm 122; 1 Corinthians 9-11
- ❏ November 12 . . . . Job 37-38; 1 Corinthians 12
- ❏ November 13 . . . . Job 39-40; 1 Corinthians 13-14
- ❏ November 14 . . . . Psalm 149; 1 Corinthians 15-16
- ❏ November 15 . . . . Job 41-42; 2 Corinthians 1-2
- ❏ November 16 . . . . 2 Corinthians 3-6
- ❏ November 17 . . . . 2 Corinthians 7-10
- ❏ November 18 . . . . Psalm 124; 2 Corinthians 11-13
- ❏ November 19 . . . . Matthew 1-4
- ❏ November 20 . . . . Matthew 5-7
- ❏ November 21 . . . . Matthew 8-10
- ❏ November 22 . . . . Matthew 11-13
- ❏ November 23 . . . . Matthew 14-16
- ❏ November 24 . . . . Matthew 17-19
- ❏ November 25 . . . . Matthew 20-22
- ❏ November 26 . . . . Matthew 23-25
- ❏ November 27 . . . . Psalm 125; Matthew 26-27
- ❏ November 28 . . . . Matthew 28; 1 Thessalonians 1-3
- ❏ November 29 . . . . 1 Thessalonians 4-5; 2 Thessalonians 1-3
- ❏ November 30 . . . . Romans 1-4
- ❏ December 1 . . . . Romans 5-8
- ❏ December 2 . . . . Romans 9-12
- ❏ December 3 . . . . Romans 13-16
- ❏ December 4 . . . . Ephesians 1-4
- ❏ December 5 . . . . Ephesians 5-6; Psalm 119:1-80
- ❏ December 6 . . . . Philippians 1-4
- ❏ December 7 . . . . Colossians 1-4
- ❏ December 8 . . . . 1 Timothy 1-4
- ❏ December 9 . . . . 1 Timothy 5-6; Titus 1-3
- ❏ December 10 . . . . 2 Timothy 1-4

DATE	SCRIPTURE READING
❏ December 11	Philemon; Hebrews 1–4
❏ December 12	Hebrews 5–8
❏ December 13	Hebrews 9–11
❏ December 14	Hebrews 12–13; Jude
❏ December 15	James 1–5
❏ December 16	1 Peter 1–5
❏ December 17	2 Peter 1–3; John 1
❏ December 18	John 2–4
❏ December 19	John 5–6
❏ December 20	John 7–8
❏ December 21	John 9–11
❏ December 22	John 12–14
❏ December 23	John 15–18
❏ December 24	John 19–21
❏ December 25	1 John 1–5
❏ December 26	Psalm 117, 119:81–176; 2 John; 3 John
❏ December 27	Revelation 1–4
❏ December 28	Revelation 5–9
❏ December 29	Revelation 10–14
❏ December 30	Revelation 15–18
❏ December 31	Revelation 19–22

GET CLOSER

JANUARY 1-7

WEEK 1

A SINGLE SACRIFICE

But when Christ had offered for all time a single sacrifice for sins, he sat down at the right hand of God, waiting from that time until his enemies should be made a footstool for his feet. For by a single offering, he has perfected for all time those who are being sanctified.

—HEBREWS 10:12-14 (ESV)

IN THE OLD Testament, God required animal sacrifices to atone for man's sins—the things they did that directly went against His law. God's people, the Israelites, routinely offered these sacrifices as a way of cleansing themselves before Him. The problem was that no matter how many animals were sacrificed—no matter how much blood had been spilled, the relationship between God and man was never fully restored. These offerings were a foreshadowing, a sign, of the ultimate sacrifice, which was to come.

Then came Jesus Christ: God in the flesh. The Bible calls Jesus the "Lamb of God, who takes away the sin of the world" (John 1:29). The reality is that man's sins are too great for him to atone for himself. No act, no sacrifice, of man is enough to wipe his ledger clean before God. This is why God Himself had to come and pay the price.

When Jesus died on the cross, His shed blood was the single sacrifice that forever paid the penalty for sin. This is why Hebrews says that Christ "perfected for all time" those who call on His name. Rather than continual offerings, the New

Testament holds the amazing news that the debt has been paid in full! Those who put their faith in Jesus' name—His life, death, and resurrection—don't need to fret or be anxious about the status of their relationship with God. They are forever secure and forever righteous because of the work of Jesus!

Do you struggle to believe that there's nothing more you can do to add to Jesus' salvation? Do you find yourself striving to earn God's approval and justify yourself before Him? Remember, Jesus finished the work! You can rest in the eternal security that comes through faith in Him. Thanks to His single sacrifice, we are perfected in God's eyes! That's news worth celebrating today.

APPLICATION QUESTIONS

1) Do you find it easy or difficult to trust that Jesus' work on the cross seals your salvation? Why do you think this is?

2) In Leviticus chapters 1-7, God gives the Israelites instructions for bringing different kinds of offerings before Him: burnt offerings, grain offerings, sin offerings, guilt offerings, ordination offerings, and peace offerings. Skim through these chapters and take note of the different circumstances under which the people were required to make sacrifices. How did Jesus' death and resurrection forever change how we come before the Lord?

3) Take time in prayer to thank God for the immeasurable gift of His Son and the eternal salvation He purchased for us. Ask Him to increase your faith in His finished work, so you can trust and rest in Him!

JANUARY 8-14

WEEK 2

MENTORING OTHERS

"Listen, O Israel! The LORD is our God, the LORD alone. And you must love the LORD your God with all your heart, all your soul, and all your strength. And you must commit yourselves wholeheartedly to these commands that I am giving you today. Repeat them again and again to your children. Talk about them when you are at home and when you are on the road, when you are going to bed and when you are getting up. Tie them to your hands and wear them on your forehead as reminders. Write them on the doorposts of your house and on your gates."

—DEUTERONOMY 6:4-9 (NLT)

FROM THE OLD Testament times all the way through Jesus' day, Jewish children were heavily steeped in the Law of the Lord. Their education consisted of memorizing massive portions of the Scripture. Some of these children grew up to become scribes, painstakingly copying passages of the Law over and over again. During worship gatherings and feasts, the Word of God was read aloud. Faithful parents and mentors continually taught younger generations the truths that had been revealed through prophets and judges and kings.

Today, God also calls us to share His truth with those younger (both in age and in the faith) than us. Whether you're single, married, a parent, a mentor—no matter your season in life—there are individuals in your life who are hungry for the Word. Do we know the truth well enough to continually share it with others?

You don't have to be a Bible scholar to do this. As we see in the Deuteronomy passage above, sometimes sharing the Word can be as simple as a conversation during a car ride or a mealtime discussion. Ask God to show you the mundane moments throughout your day when you can study His Word and pour into the next generation. Your actions may have an impact for generations to come!

APPLICATION QUESTIONS

1) What does your current Scripture-reading routine look like? How often do you delve into the Word of God right now?

2) Who are some younger individuals in your life whom you can mentor in the faith? What might these exchanges look like on a daily basis?

3) What concerns, questions, or fears are holding you back from sharing God's truth with others? Take some time to bring these reservations before the Lord and ask for His help in stepping past them.

JANUARY 15-21

WEEK 3

ALL SHE HAD

Jesus sat down opposite the place where the offerings were put and watched the crowd putting their money into the temple treasury. Many rich people threw in large amounts. But a poor widow came and put in two very small copper coins, worth only a few cents. Calling his disciples to him, Jesus said, "Truly I tell you, this poor widow has put more into the treasury than all the others. They all gave out of their wealth; but she, out of her poverty, put in everything—all she had to live on."

—MARK 12:41-44 (NIV)

A BIG DEBATE in the church today centers around tithing: How much should we give to God? What percentage of our income can we "afford" to offer to Him? While this discussion is important, we often approach it with the wrong mindset: a perspective that assumes we have something to give to God in the first place.

James 1:17 tells us that every single good gift we have comes from the Father. Psalm 24:1-2 reminds us that everything in the world belongs to the Lord. We don't truly "own" anything for ourselves; rather, God entrusts us with resources, belongings, and gifts to use for His glory. Since this is the truth, we should approach the giving debate with the mindset of surrendering to the Lord what is already His.

The amount that each person decides to give is unique to himself or herself. 2 Corinthians 9:8 (NIV) tells us, "Each man should give what he has decided in his heart to give, not reluctantly or under compulsion, for God loves a cheerful giver." The percentage that you tithe, offer, or give generously to God is between you and God, but keep in mind that, really, everything you have is the Lord's to begin with—He's simply asking you to trust Him with it.

How can you use your time, resources, and gifts to glorify God? What area of your life needs to be fully surrendered to Him? What "two copper coins" might you be withholding from Him?

APPLICATION QUESTIONS

1) Do you currently have a certain percentage, or amount, of your income that you tithe or give to the church? Why or why not?

2) What nonmaterial skills, gifts, or resources do you want to more fully surrender to the Lord? How might He be asking you to use these resources?

3) What makes it difficult for you to fully surrender your resources to the Lord? Take some time in prayer and thank God for His abundant blessings and for trusting you to steward them. Ask for His help in this stewardship journey—that He would reorient your perspective to match His own.

JANUARY 22-28

WEEK 4

BODY AND SPIRIT

Have nothing to do with godless myths and old wives' tales; rather, train yourself to be godly. For physical training is of some value, but godliness has value for all things, holding promise for both the present life and the life to come. This is a trustworthy saying that deserves full acceptance.

—1 TIMOTHY 4:7-9 (NIV)

GOD NEVER INTENDED for us to be merely physical beings; likewise, we aren't only spiritual in nature. There's a multifaceted nature to our makeup. Some people lean too far towards the physical side of things, neglecting spiritual disciplines and matters of faith.

Often, however, in the church, we can lean so far towards the spiritual things that we neglect our minds and bodies. This passage, written by Paul to Timothy, affirms the importance—however small—of physical training. It is important to stay fit and healthy—to train one's body and mind through exercise and healthy habits. However, this physical training is secondary in importance to godliness.

How do we maintain a balance between these two parts of ourselves? By understanding that they aren't separated at all. The Bible says that God created us—mind, body, and spirit. He has given us our bodies, and we should aim to honor Him with how we use them. Likewise, God is the One we need in order to be spiritually healthy. His Word is the key to growing in our faith and in our spiritual maturity. So even our physical exercise can be a spiritual discipline; likewise, growing closer to God can help us better steward our bodies and our minds.

This week, as you seek to become more like Jesus, ask yourself what physical ramifications this might have in your life. What about spiritual outcomes? Challenge yourself to see these two as related, not opposing or separated. At the same time, remember that when it comes down to it, our physical bodies won't go with us to heaven, so ensure that your pursuit of God is first and foremost in your priorities.

APPLICATION QUESTIONS

1) Do you tend to focus more on your physical health or on your spiritual health? Why do you think this is?

2) Think about the fitness you focus on the least. What's one step you can take to begin improving your health in this area?

3) In your own words, explain the relationship between physical and spiritual fitness. Which one is more important to God? How can you integrate both into your life while still keeping first things first?

JANUARY 29 – FEBRUARY 4

WEEK 5

MANDATORY FUN!

The Lord said to Moses, "Speak to the Israelites and say to them: 'These are my appointed festivals, the appointed festivals of the Lord, which you are to proclaim as sacred assemblies. There are six days when you may work, but the seventh day is a day of sabbath rest, a day of sacred assembly. You are not to do any work; wherever you live, it is a sabbath to the Lord.'"

—LEVITICUS 23:1-3 (NIV)

GOD HIMSELF APPOINTED festivals and feasts periodically throughout the year for His people. He could have simply said, "Look at all I've done for you. You'd better work hard each and every day to make it up to me. Days off? Give Me a break." Instead, He not only encourages relaxation and fun—He *mandates* it.

The Israelites observed multiple holidays, including one every single week. The Sabbath day is a fairly well-known commandment. But how faithfully do we keep it today? In an era of remote work, constant online content, and very little margin to "unplug," it's unlikely many of us enjoy a day of complete rest and communion with God. More likely, we're grasping at twelve minutes here, an hour there, four minutes in the car on the way to pick up the kids from school. . . .

Now think about the little pockets of rest in your life. How many of them are you spending with the Lord? This could be reading the Word, simply talking to Him, lifting up others in prayer, or inviting Him into the restful rhythms of your life. If we're honest with ourselves, we tend to get lost in TV shows, music, socializing with others, or the list we're making for what we need to do *after* we get out of bed.

This week, challenge yourself—and ask for God's help—to rededicate your downtime. All of us can make time to feast, to rest, to relax. We have it somewhere in our schedule. The key is dedicating it to God first. The more we do that, the more miraculous rest time we'll find! God can take and multiply our rest—in fact, throughout the Word, He promises us rest in Himself! Stop looking for reprieve in entertainment and others. These things are good, but go to God first. Ask Him to teach you how to Sabbath again, how to celebrate and feast again. Go against the grain of the culture of this world and take a deep breath. It's not just a suggestion—it's a requirement!

APPLICATION QUESTIONS

1) What do you think it says about God's character that He included rest in the Ten Commandments?

2) Where do we see Jesus taking time to rest with the Father during His earthly life?

3) What's one thing you can give up this week and trade for restful time with God? What might this time look like? Remember, it doesn't have to be only reading your Bible—think of creative ways to unwind with your Creator (art journaling, worship music in the car, or even prayer and a nap are great options)!

FEBRUARY 5-11

WEEK 6

A ROMAN'S FAITH

When he had entered Capernaum, a centurion came forward to him, appealing to him, "Lord, my servant is lying paralyzed at home, suffering terribly." And he said to him, "I will come and heal him." But the centurion replied, "Lord, I am not worthy to have you come under my roof, but only say the word, and my servant will be healed. For I too am a man under authority, with soldiers under me. And I say to one, 'Go,' and he goes, and to another, 'Come,' and he comes, and to my servant, 'Do this,' and he does it." When Jesus heard this, he marveled and said to those who followed him, "Truly, I tell you, with no one in Israel have I found such faith."

—MATTHEW 8:5-10 (ESV)

IT WAS FAITH for the centurion to even approach Jesus. But he didn't stop there. Most people in Jesus' day wanted to see signs—they followed Him in hopes that He'd feed another five thousand, heal their sick, and make their lives better. However, it was clear who was there for a show and who was there because they believed that Jesus was the Messiah.

This centurion was part of the Roman empire. He wasn't a Jew, and he wasn't of the Jewish faith. However, he'd heard stories about Jesus. Not only did he need a miracle for his servant, though that would have been a good reason to come to Jesus on its own. But watch what he says: "Don't come to my house, Jesus. I'm not *worthy*." This in a time when the Roman empire was taking over the known world, subjecting the Jews to their laws. Often, the religious orders of the Jews and the Romans would clash about laws and statutes (we see this happen when Jesus is crucified). But here, we see a mighty Roman centurion humbly ask Jesus for help.

What faith must he have had in the Jewish carpenter from Nazareth! The centurion's unique position gave him an understanding of authority. He knew it wasn't about Jesus' appearance, nationality, or resume. It was about His position.

Do we recognize the authority of Jesus in our own lives? Do we humbly submit to His plans? Do we trust that even if it doesn't look like we expect, He can do miracles for us? Jesus had glowing words for the centurion for trusting Him: "With no one in Israel have I found such faith." As God's children, let us have this kind of faith. Let it not be said of us that we didn't trust the Lord to do things in His way, in His timing.

Even though this centurion's encounter with Jesus was brief, it had repercussions that lasted years into the future. That's what God can do when we place our faith in Him!

APPLICATION QUESTIONS

1) How do you think Jesus' followers felt when He said that the centurion's faith was greater than any He'd found in Israel? What lesson do you think Jesus wanted them to learn from the centurion's example?

2) Are there any expectations you have for how God works in your life? How might He want to challenge those expectations? How might your faith need to grow in those areas?

3) The centurion left Jesus, and the Bible tells us the servant was healed at that very moment. However, the centurion couldn't have known this until he returned home. How can this story inform the faith you have in God, even when His answers to your prayers aren't immediately apparent?

FEBRUARY 12-18

WEEK 7

ADOPTING A SPIRIT OF HONOR

"Respect your father and your mother, as I, the Lord your God, command you, so that all may go well with you and so that you may live a long time in the land that I am giving you."
—DEUTERONOMY 5:16 (GNT)

MANY OF US have heard this passage before, but did you know that the word "honor" carries a weightiness, a significance, that is often overlooked? We may assume that honoring someone means obeying them, but this isn't the connotation given by Deuteronomy 5:16. While obedience is many times part of honoring authority, it's not the only part.

Honoring someone is respecting them, giving weight to their position and their decisions. It's showing humility in how you interact with them, understanding that God has placed them in their role for a purpose. In the same way that we honor local authorities, we are called to honor our parents. We may not always agree with their judgment calls. We may have trouble seeing them as role models or authority figures over us.

But regardless of what our parents' lives look like, the decisions they've made, or the ways in which they've failed us, the Bible is clear: We are to honor them. We are to show respect, even if they are not respectful towards us. This has less to do with who they are and more to do with the posture of our hearts toward God. After all, if we can't accept the first people He has placed over us and show them respect, how will we be able to respect others in authority?

Our parents are our first lesson in honor. Sometimes, it's a hard lesson. This week, brainstorm ways you can begin to change the posture of your heart towards your parents. Remember everything they've done for you despite their shortcomings. Adopt a posture of gratitude and respect as you think of them. Ask the Holy Spirit to show you concrete ways to honor them—even if you'll never fully be on the same page.

APPLICATION QUESTIONS

1) Do a quick internet search on this verse and the word "honor." In your own words, what does the Hebrew term mean? How does this change your view of the passage?

2) Do you find it easy or difficult to honor your parents? Dive a little deeper into your answer. What are some of the factors behind it?

3) What's one or two ways you can begin to show your parents honor this week? Is it a text saying thank you? A commitment not to continue old arguments? A small gift?

FEBRUARY 19-25

WEEK 8

FAITHFUL STEWARDSHIP

His master said to him, "Well done, good and faithful servant. You have been faithful over a little; I will set you over much. Enter into the joy of your master."
—MATTHEW 25:23 (ESV)

THE PARABLE OF the Talents is one of the most commonly known lessons Jesus gave about stewardship. While the parable dealt with finances specifically, it also spoke to how we steward all of the resources, gifts, and talents God has given us. Since this week's subject is finances, however, let's take a direct look at what the two faithful servants did that the unfaithful servant did not.

Matthew 25 tells us that the first two servants were given different amounts of money to start with before the master went away on his journey. The first servant was given five talents, and the second servant was given two. Rather than compare or complain or question the master's judgment, the servants got to work quickly, doubling their respective amounts.

They knew their master well enough to know what his expectations were. This likely wasn't their first time managing his belongings. Upon the master's return, they were ready with a report, the doubled amounts in hand. They weren't caught empty-handed or in the middle of a long transaction. They had been efficient and orderly about their investments, prepared for the return of their master.

They are both deemed faithful servants, not because of the amounts they were entrusted with, but because they stewarded them well. Are we prepared to do the same?

Do we know our Master well enough to understand what He expects us to do with the things He's given us? Do we have a strategic plan for how to use these resources? Are we prepared at all times to give an account, in case the Lord returns? Are we living in expectation and wisdom with the finances we have?

This week, take some time to reflect on your financial situation. Maybe your next step is reaching out to someone for advice on how to get ahead financially. Maybe it's finding an accountability partner. Maybe it's taking a risk and giving to a cause the Lord is drawing your heart towards. No matter what the Holy Spirit convicts you to do next, commit your finances to Him, and remember that He has entrusted them to you. They are His after all.

APPLICATION QUESTIONS

1) Do you struggle with comparing your financial situation to others'? Why or why not?

2) What's that next step in stewarding your finances well? What's holding you back or making it more difficult to take that step?

3) Who can you invite into your financial situation to provide encouragement, accountability, and wisdom? Text, call, or meet up with that person this week!

FEBRUARY 26–MARCH 4

WEEK 9

BOUGHT WITH A PRICE

Or do you not know that your body is a temple of the Holy Spirit within you, whom you have from God, and that you are not your own? For you have been bought for a price: therefore glorify God in your body.
—1 CORINTHIANS 6:19-20 (NASB)

THE HARDEST THING about this passage for most of us, is that we tend to think of our body as our own property. After all, the culture we live in tells us that it's our right to do with our bodies whatever we want. We understand healthy physical boundaries with others—that it's not all right to cross lines and violate the bodies of others.

However, have you considered that your body doesn't belong to you? That God created it and is redeeming it through the redemptive work of Jesus Christ? Though we still struggle with earthly sicknesses and limitations, there will come a day when our bodies will be restored and made perfect once again.

Paul writes to the Corinthian church in the context of sexual sins that were happening among the body of believers. Not only does the concept of God owning our bodies extend to physical fitness—it applies to everything we do with our bodies: eating, drinking, sex, exercise, work, and so much more.

The Corinthian church had instances of incest, unions with pagan temple prostitutes, and other sexual sins. Sounds a bit like our world today, doesn't it? Paul reminded these young believers that these sins were exactly the sins Jesus died for on the cross! They'd been bought spiritually, set free, and redeemed. They needed to start living in light of that.

Whether our misconduct with our bodies is sexual, whether it relates to laziness, or whether we simply haven't been giving thought to how we use our bodies in light of God's salvation, now is the time to repent and ask Him to remove these sins from our lives. This week may be a difficult awakening for you, but press in. Spend time in prayer and the Word. Allow the Lord to reveal the areas in which you haven't fully submitted your mind and body to Him.

APPLICATION QUESTIONS

1) What sins are you currently struggling with as they relate to your mind and body? Can you find any Scripture references that speak to these sins?

2) How does the concept that you were "bought with a price" go against the cultural idea that your body is completely yours and that you're free to do whatever you want with it?

3) What might be some positive outcomes of surrendering the areas you listed above to God, and allowing His truth to direct your physical actions? How might they affect your life? Your health? Those around you?

MARCH 5-11

WEEK 10

EVEN MORE UNDIGNIFIED

Then King David was told, "The Lord has blessed Obed-edom's household and everything he has because of the Ark of God." So David went there and brought the Ark of God from the house of Obed-edom to the City of David with a great celebration. After the men who were carrying the Ark of the Lord had gone six steps, David sacrificed a bull and a fattened calf. And David danced before the Lord with all his might, wearing a priestly garment. So David and all the people of Israel brought up the Ark of the Lord with shouts of joy and the blowing of rams' horns.

—2 SAMUEL 6:12-15 (NLT)

AN INTERESTING POINT in this story to note is that Michal, David's wife, saw him dancing before the ark from a high window. After this passage, the Bible tells us that she confronted him about it. Apparently, it was an undignified way to worship in her opinion. David replied, "I will celebrate before the Lord! And I might demean myself even more than this and be lowly in my own sight, but with the female slaves of whom you have spoken, with them I am to be held in honor!"

What an interesting response. Instead of catering to the cultural expectations of the day, David celebrated and became undignified in the presence of the Lord.

Many of us spend so much time worrying about how we are perceived that even in fun moments, or in the midst of celebrations, we don't feel free to be fully ourselves. We may put on a mask of sorts, or hold back from expressing ourselves creatively, fearing judgment or a hit to our reputation. But David danced for an audience of One.

The occasion was special. The ark was being carried back into Jerusalem, the city of David, after a long time away. It was a moment for wild celebration. The ark was, in that time period, the manifestation of God's presence with His people. This wasn't just another feast or party—this was a turning point for God's nation. David didn't hold back, and God honored him for his worship.

It comes down to motivation: are we worshiping and having fun so that others will see us? Are their opinions foremost in our minds? Or are we basing our activities and our celebrations around what God thinks? Apply this to the celebrations and times of enjoyment in your life this week. Whose approval are you most after?

APPLICATION QUESTIONS

1) Do you find it difficult to be fully authentic in front of others when you celebrate or have fun? Explain your answer.

2) What do you think is holding you back from worshiping and having fun in an uninhibited way? Are there any opinions or expectations that hold you back?

3) Ask the Lord to help you focus more on Him than on others and to fully engage in the things that bring you life and bring honor to Him. What are some of the things He may be asking you to step into? A new hobby? An artistic form of worship? Letting go of insecurities?

MARCH 12-18

WEEK 11

THE WAITING GAME

He took him outside and said, "Look up at the sky and count the stars—if indeed you can count them." Then he said to him, "So shall your offspring be." Abram believed the Lord, and he credited it to him as righteousness.

—GENESIS 15:5-6 (NIV)

ABRAM—OR ABRAHAM, as he was later renamed by God—is one of the greatest examples of steadfast faith in the Bible. From leaving his homeland at God's command, to receiving this promise and believing the Lord, to waiting *decades* for the fulfillment of the promise, to later being willing to sacrifice his son, Isaac, in order to be obedient, Abraham had a life full of expectant faith in God.

One aspect of his life that we don't often spend too much time thinking about is the extremely long waiting period between the promise of a son and the birth of that son. Abraham was seventy-five years old when God first promised that Isaac would be born. In addition to that long life, Abraham waited *twenty-five more years* before the arrival of his promised offspring. Imagine the long weeks and months that transpired in those twenty-five years. Imagine the hope, the frustration, the disappointment, the confusion, perhaps, that Abraham felt.

Abraham's wife, Sarah, also waited. As the years went by, it probably got harder to believe that a pregnancy and birth was possible for the couple. They noticed their bodies changing with the years, their intimacy not exactly what it had been. Imagine the number of times that the thought must have crossed Abraham's mind—just like Satan introduced it to Adam and Eve in the garden: "Did God *really* say. . . ?"

Yet we see an unwavering faith from Abraham. He knew who his God was. He trusted, even when years went by between reiterations of the promise. He maintained faith in God not because of what Abraham was capable of in himself, but because he knew that God could do anything.

Maybe today you're waiting on a promise from God to be fulfilled. Maybe you're waiting for the promise to be articulated in the first place! Maybe you've rejoiced at the fulfillment of a promise and can testify to seeing the other side of the waiting period. No matter where you are, take time today to ask God for increased faith. Ask Him to reorient your heart and mind on His abilities, not the circumstances around you or your own strength.

Let's be inspired by Abraham today, and thank God for empowering us to trust in Him, even during the silent, waiting years.

APPLICATION QUESTIONS

1) Have you ever received a promise from God and then seen it fulfilled? Share about this experience. If you can't think of any specific promises, find a promise from God's Word and write it below. How does this promise apply to you personally?

2) What makes it difficult for you to believe in God's promises during those quiet, waiting times? What doubts, critical thoughts, or circumstances make it difficult to keep the faith?

3) Why do you think it was so important that Abraham believed God, instead of believing in himself? How can you shift your faith so that it rests in God's ability and not your own? Are there any action steps that can help you make this shift?

MARCH 19-25

WEEK 12

KIDS TODAY...

Children, obey your parents in the Lord, for this is right. "Honor your father and mother," which is the first commandment with promise: "that it may be well with you and you may live long on the earth." And you, fathers, do not provoke your children to wrath, but bring them up in the training and admonition of the Lord.
—EPHESIANS 6:1-4 (NKJV)

WE'VE ALREADY TAKEN a look at the passage that instructs children to honor their parents in a previous week. This week, consider how the passage above instructs *all* family members to honor one another. Often, we hear about the importance of children's obedience and respect towards their elders. But did you know that God commands adults to respect and cherish children, as well?

Here, Paul writes to the Ephesians. In previous chapters, he encouraged the believers to put on Christ's righteousness, like new clothes, instead of their own sinful nature. Throughout the letter, Paul explained how this looks in every area of life: community, marriage, family, and more. By the time we get to chapter 6, it's clear that the family is an essential representation to the world of God's love and restorative power. After mentioning the child-parent relationship, Paul then went on to talk about slaves and masters as well.

The key in this passage is that we interact with and love our family, friends, coworkers, and communities not because they are necessarily deserving. After all, we know that parents aren't perfect, children don't need to be taught how to lie or misbehave, and cruel bosses and slave masters certainly don't deserve respect. Instead, we treat others with honor and respect because we're showing a fallen world what the power of the Holy Spirit looks like in us. Instead of giving in to anger and frustration, fathers (and mothers) are called to train their children up in the ways of the Lord. One of the most important ways we can teach those younger than us (either our own children or those who are younger in the faith than we are) is to *model* the character qualities and principles we want them to inherit. It doesn't mean much if we tell children to be patient and never show them what patience looks like, does it?

If you're a parent, use this week to take a step back and evaluate how you're doing in this area. Do you show honor and respect to your children? Do you listen to them, even when it's hard? Do you take an interest in their world? Jesus does. If you don't have children, think of the younger members of your church or community who need your influence and encouragement. How can you honor and respect them? It's difficult to relate to other generations, but here we see a call to do just that. Just as younger individuals are called to heed their elders, adults are called to pour into the next generation, raising them up in the knowledge and fear of the Lord.

Someone poured into you when you were younger. Now, it's your turn. Who around you needs to be honored, respected, encouraged, and invested in?

APPLICATION QUESTIONS

1) Think about someone who was a formative influence in your younger years. What specific words, actions, and lifestyles did this person display that made a difference to you?

2) Think about the children, siblings, church members, coworkers, or schoolmates in your life who are younger than you. List 2 to 3 people below that you can pour into more intentionally.

3) How can you begin to model Jesus to the younger generation? What words, actions, and lifestyle changes might this entail?

MARCH 26 – APRIL 1

WEEK 13

MORE THAN A MORTGAGE

And he told them this parable: "*The ground of a certain rich man yielded an abundant harvest. He thought to himself,* What shall I do? I have no place to store my crops. *Then he said,* 'This is what I'll do. I will tear down my barns and build bigger ones, and there I will store my surplus grain. And I'll say to myself, You have plenty of grain laid up for many years. Take life easy; eat, drink and be merry.' *But God said to him,* "You fool! This very night your life will be demanded from you. Then who will get what you have prepared for yourself?" *This is how it will be with whoever stores up things for themselves but is not rich toward God.*

—LUKE 12:16-21 (NIV)

IS THE MORAL of this story that it's wrong to upsize, or to build a bigger house when you run out of room? Not exactly.

The parable Jesus tells his disciples in this passage has to do with the desire to be secure in one's own strength, instead of trusting in God. In Luke 12:1-12, Jesus instructs His followers not to be afraid of earthly dangers and trials because the Father sees them and cares for them. Even in the future, when persecution would come to His followers, Jesus assures them that the Holy Spirit will provide them words to speak. They don't need to worry about it.

This passage is immediately followed by a request from someone in the crowd, who asks Jesus to make his brother divide the family inheritance evenly between the two of them. Jesus responds, "You there—who appointed Me a judge or arbitrator over the two of you. . . ? Beware, and be on your guard against every form of greed, for not even when one is affluent does his life consist of his possessions." Then, he goes into the parable of the rich fool who built his bigger barns.

Clearly, property and wealth aren't the culprits here. Instead, it's the spirit of entitlement and pride that says, "I don't need God! I can do this myself. I can build my own empire and earn my own security!" It's the same spirit that Lucifer had when he rebelled against God. No matter how much we have, it's too much if we put our ultimate trust in ourselves and our achievements.

Think about all that God has blessed you with. Chances are you have a home, a mode of transportation, and adequate financial income. Hopefully, you're physically healthy right now, and you're able to read this sentence and understand it. There are so many blessings that we take for granted, or believe that we've earned with our own efforts. This week, give credit where it's due: praise God for sustaining you, providing for you, and being with you always.

It's not a sin to have things or to be wealthy. It's a sin to trust in wealth instead of in God.

APPLICATION QUESTIONS

1) What are some of the material blessings that God has given to you?

2) How might it be easy to trust in these material blessings and find ultimate security in them?

3) How can you possess these blessings and still maintain ultimate faith and security in God? What might this look like practically? What might you need to surrender or loosen your hold on in order for this to happen?

APRIL 2-8

WEEK 14

STILL KICKING

"And now behold, the Lord has let me live, just as He spoke, these forty-five years, from the time that the Lord spoke this word to Moses, when Israel walked in the wilderness; and now behold, I am eighty-five years old today. I am still as strong today as I was on the day Moses sent me; as my strength was then, so my strength is now, for war and for going out and coming in. Now then, give me this hill country about which the Lord spoke on that day, for you heard on that day that Anakim were there, with great fortified cities; perhaps the Lord will be with me, and I will drive them out just as the Lord has spoken."

—JOSHUA 14:10-12 (NASB)

OF THE TWELVE Israelite spies that went into the Promised Land to scout out the area, only two had confidence that they could overcome it with God's protection. Joshua and Caleb gave a positive report upon returning from their mission, while the other ten spies caved in to cowardice and fear. Because the majority of the people didn't trust God to follow through on His word, the Israelites were punished with another forty years wandering in the wilderness.

At the end of this forty years, we come to this passage, in which a new generation of God's people are finally ready to trust Him and take the land of Canaan for their own possession. Joshua spoke to the people as one of only two men who were alive during that first expedition who remained. He said, "I'm still as strong as the day I went into the land for the first time." Isn't that amazing? Through God's power and his own obedience,

Joshua's physical fitness, at eighty-five years old, is greater than many people much younger than him!

Not only was it essential for Joshua to trust God and remain obedient; we also see the importance of his readiness to fight for and claim his piece of the Promised Land. Our physical fitness may be less important than our spiritual fitness, but the two go hand-in-hand: in order to carry out the work God has given us, we need to be physically healthy. How can we share the gospel, meet the needs of others, and display the strength of our God if we aren't healthy—if our own basic needs are not met?

This week, consider how your physical fitness might be connected to the callings and purposes God has placed on your heart. What do you need to do to get your mind and body ready for the work in front of you? Is it adding in a couple of exercise sessions a week? Is it amending your diet to include more healthy ingredients? Is it as simple as staying hydrated, or going on a walk on your lunch break? Is it taking a mental health day every once in a while to reset and recharge?

These actions aren't luxuries—they're directly tied to your ability to serve the Lord. Just as Joshua's fitness empowered him to take the possession God had for him, our fitness is essential to moving forward in our walk with the Lord.

APPLICATION QUESTIONS

1) How has God already sustained you physically and mentally? How has He kept you strong?

2) What's your responsibility in maintaining your fitness? What do you need to do to partner with God in keeping yourself healthy?

3) How might your fitness (or lack thereof) affect the purposes and the assignments that God has given you? What might happen if you're not healthy enough to complete the tasks ahead of you?

APRIL 9-15

WEEK 15

A FESTIVE FAITH

> *The next day there was a wedding celebration in the village of Cana in Galilee. Jesus' mother was there, and Jesus and his disciples were also invited to the celebration. The wine supply ran out during the festivities, so Jesus' mother told him, "They have no more wine." "Dear woman, that's not our problem," Jesus replied. "My time has not yet come."*
>
> —JOHN 2:1-4 (NLT)

WE OFTEN GLOSS over the fact that Jesus attended a wedding to focus on the miracle that happened *at* the wedding. But let's not move too quickly through this passage. Before Jesus turns water into wine, he takes his disciples to a celebration. It's possible that Jesus knew the couple getting married, or that they were friends of one of his disciples or Mary, his mother. After all, Cana was only a handful of miles away from Nazareth, Jesus' hometown.

In Jesus' day, it was customary for wedding celebrations to go on for several days. That means that, before the miracle, wine would have flowed freely during this time. Dancing was also customary at celebrations of this kind. It's likely that Jesus and his disciples took part in the festivities, too!

We don't often think about Jesus having fun, per se. Many of the stories we find in Scripture involve miracles, teachings, and the opposition that our Lord faced. However, Jesus spent thirty-three years on earth—three whole years of which were spent with his disciples. We really only see glimpses of his life throughout these years. There are many traditions, feasts, and fun moments that we don't get to see. But Jesus' presence at this wedding is one of the rare times we saw him attend a celebration. He probably drank wine. He probably laughed. He probably interacted with children. He probably danced.

Make time this week to breathe deeply, enjoy a good meal, listen to your favorite music, or invite those you love to do something completely recreational in nature. Maybe you like to be outdoors—if so, go for a hike or a swim or a jog. Play your favorite game. Read a book you've been putting off for a while. Host a karaoke party. Show off your dance moves.

If the Lord of the universe thought it necessary and good to rest—to have fun, to celebrate with his friends—why shouldn't we?

APPLICATION QUESTIONS

1) How does the picture of Jesus enjoying a wedding change your perspective of His personality?

2) What are some things you enjoy doing solely for the fun of it? Are there any of these things you haven't done in a long time? What's holding you back?

3) Who can you invite to join you in these activities this week? Chances are, they'll be glad you asked!

APRIL 16-22

WEEK 16

A SYMPATHETIC HIGH PRIEST

Then he said to them, "My soul is very sorrowful, even to death; remain here, and watch with me." And going a little farther he fell on his face and prayed, saying, "My Father, if it be possible, let this cup pass from me; nevertheless, not as I will, but as you will."

—MATTHEW 26:38-39 (ESV)

IT'S COMMON TO assume that having great faith means that obeying God is easy. *If I have faith,* we may think, *I won't be tempted to go my own way. It'll be second nature to yield to God's will.* While this can be true many times, we can't equate faith with an easy walk. If anyone had faith, it was the Son of God Himself. Yet we see, on the last night of Jesus' earthly life, He grappled and struggled with the choice ahead of Him.

Would He obey the Father, and submit to an excruciating, torturous death on the cross? Or would He choose to avoid the unthinkable pain and find a way out? He was still fully God: He could call legions of angels down to free Him at any time (Matthew 26:53). But He didn't. This passage of scripture is essential for us to grasp as believers, because it displays Christ's humanity. It wasn't easy for Him to choose the cross. The Bible tells us that he sweat great drops of blood. He was mentally, physically, and emotionally agonized over this decision. No one loved the Father more than Jesus, but here, even Jesus asked for a reprieve. He asked to be allowed not to go through with the plan. He asked not to have to do what He had come to do.

The encouraging part of this account isn't just that Jesus struggled as we do; it's that He yielded in the end. Despite the temptation to avoid His calling, He prayed, "Not as I will, but as you will." Because Christ was obedient, you and I have the power of the Holy Spirit, by which we can say the same thing. When obedience is hard—agonizing, even—we can know that Jesus sympathizes with us. He, too, struggled to say "yes" to God. We can also rest assured that it's possible to surrender, because He did, too.

Is there something God is asking you to do that seems unbearably hard? Are you in the midst of giving up something in order to walk in obedience? You're not alone. Jesus knows how it feels to go against your human nature; He knows how hard it is to surrender when everything in you is screaming at you to avoid the discomfort, the pain. Be encouraged today: you have a High Priest who sympathizes with your weakness, was tempted in every way, and yet did not sin (Hebrews 4:15). He made a way for us to do the same. Let's praise Him for that this week!

APPLICATION QUESTIONS

1) How does it make you feel to know that even Jesus struggled to submit to God's will?

2) Is there anything difficult that God is calling you to right now? What makes it hard to submit to His will in this area?

3) Read Hebrews 4:14-16. In your own words, how does Jesus' obedience empower us to be obedient?

APRIL 23-29

WEEK 17

FATHER DAUGHTER PROBLEMS

Before Lot and his guests could go to bed, every man in Sodom, young and old, came and stood outside his house and started shouting, "Where are your visitors? Send them out, so we can have sex with them!" Lot went outside and shut the door behind him. Then he said, "Friends, please don't do such a terrible thing! I have two daughters who have never been married. I'll bring them out, and you can do what you want with them. But don't harm these men. They are guests in my home."

—GENESIS 19:4-8 (CEV)

HERE WE SEE a prime example of how *not* to care for your family. Lot was the nephew of Abraham and had recently parted ways with him due to an overcrowding of their lands. Abraham went one way, and Lot went the other. As it turns out, Lot's direction held some of the most depraved cities and peoples of that time. He came to settle in a land called Sodom, known for its sexual depravity and sinful culture.

When two angels visited Lot, he showed the customary hospitality and invited them to stay in his house rather than in the town square. Lot knew that they could easily be attacked and harmed if they were out in the open. However, this is where Lot's hospitality goes a step too far. When the men of the city come and request to see the two visitors, Lot makes a horrifying offer: "Leave my guests alone in exchange for my daughters." Did you catch the statement he makes? "Do what you want with them." What father could be so negligent and cruel? In an effort to show respect to God, Lot tries to surrender his own family up to these predators.

One of the essential truths about family in the Bible is that family protects one another. Whether the family is blood family, as was the case here, or spiritual family, like Jesus and His disciples, the principle is the same. Again and again throughout Scripture, we see people of God standing in the gap for one another, staying loyal despite persecutions and imprisonments, and being willing to suffer alongside one another for a common goal. Lot shows us the alternative when fear and cowardice get in the way of his duties as a father.

Lot was still preserved and protected by God, however, and this is encouraging. Even when we fall short of our familial responsibilities, there is grace. The two angels got Lot and his family out of the city of Sodom before God destroyed it after giving them plenty of time to escape. We see that God's mercy isn't dependent on our ability to raise the perfect family or tribe, but on our faith in Him and our dependence on His Word.

Think about your family unit: maybe it's a blood family, or a family of believers, classmates, or coworkers. How can you stand by them, protect them, and show them the truth of God's Word? How can you model the Father's love in ordinary, everyday ways?

APPLICATION QUESTIONS

1) What do you think was going through Lot's mind as he desperately offered the men of the city his own daughters instead of the two heavenly guests?

2) What does your family look like? Who is in your tribe? What role do you play in this family?

3) In what ways can you improve in your love towards your family? Pray for the strength and wisdom to improve in these areas knowing that, even when you fall short, God's grace is sufficient for you (2 Corinthians 12:9-10).

APRIL 30 – MAY 6

WEEK 18

FINDING SATISFACTION

And I saw that all toil and all achievement spring from one person's envy of another. This too is meaningless, a chasing after the wind. Fools fold their hands and ruin themselves. Better one handful with tranquility than two handfuls with toil and chasing after the wind.

—ECCLESIASTES 4:4-6 (NIV)

WHY DO YOU think our culture today is so obsessed with acquiring more: more money, more property, more position, more reputation? It seems that every advertisement, social media post, and message we receive on a daily basis is oriented towards the pursuit of more. If you make more money, you can buy a bigger home. You can get a better car. You'll have a better job title. You can make more friends or have more influence. Do we ever stop to consider the downside of constantly acquiring more?

We are finite beings, after all. We have a certain amount of time, energy, and capacity. The author of Ecclesiastes, Solomon, tells us that it's better to have *just enough* and live a peaceful life than to toil and strive and have *more, more, more*. This is easy to say but harder to live out. Solomon would know. Earlier in this book, he tells the reader that he's tried the acquisition game: He's built himself lush palaces and gardens, acquired precious metals and treasures from around the world, put together a harem of the most beautiful women, and denied himself no earthly pleasure. And what is his conclusion? The refrain of Ecclesiastes is that all of it is "utterly meaningless" unless we fear God and take joy in our lot in life.

So what is Solomon's solution? Ecclesiastes 2:24 says, "A person can do nothing better than to eat and drink and find satisfaction in their own toil. This too, I see, is from the hand of God."

This week, let's pray for contentment to enjoy our work, our play, and our blessings. Instead of looking towards the next acquisition or achievement, let's thank God for the handful we have and find peace in Him. What can you thank God for today? How can you better steward what He's already given you? What haven't you appreciated enough lately? Don't look to others to tell you what to do or what to pursue. Look to God and be content with the life He's already gifted to you.

APPLICATION QUESTIONS

1) How does our culture reinforce the message that more is always better?

2) Do you find yourself struggling with always looking towards the "next thing"? What is that next thing for you? Is it a job? A material possession? A relationship?

3) What are some practical things you can do this week to rest in and enjoy the handful that God has already given you?

MAY 7-13

WEEK 19

CURBING OUR APPETITES

Then Jesus was led up by the Spirit into the wilderness to be tempted by the devil. And when He had fasted forty days and forty nights, afterward He was hungry. Now when the tempter came to Him, he said, "If You are the Son of God, command that these stones become bread." But He answered and said, "It is written, 'Man shall not live by bread alone, but by every word that proceeds from the mouth of God.'"

—MATTHEW 4:1-4 (NKJV)

FORTY DAYS WITHOUT food had left Jesus' human body weak and hungry. The enemy knew that if the Son of God would be susceptible to giving in to temptation at all, it would be at this moment. Satan's first temptation wasn't something that seems to us like it would be sinful; after all, Jesus could have easily turned the stones into bread. He had the power. He had a good reason. The offer was extremely tempting, no doubt.

So why does Jesus say no? First of all, Satan was tempting Jesus to trust in His own ability to secure provision instead of listening for the Father's permission. Jesus' fast wasn't over yet, and He never acted without consulting the Father first. Jesus was listening for "every word that proceeds from the mouth of God." This included the written Word of God, which promised that God would care for and provide for His people.

Secondly, Jesus wasn't a slave to his appetites. Though his human body experienced weakness and earthly limitations, just as ours do, He didn't allow his human frailty to dictate his actions. He was extremely hungry, but his body wasn't his master. The Father was his ultimate authority.

As we continue to explore the theme of physical fitness, this is an important principle. While listening to our bodies is essential to living healthy lives, we cannot allow our bodies to be our ultimate authority. The cravings, weaknesses, and even the strengths of our physical bodies can never supersede the truths of God's Word. If we put our ultimate faith in our physical forms, we'll be sadly disappointed when they fail us. Ultimate satisfaction can't come through any physical pleasure or strength. Jesus understood this and chose obedience to the Father over satisfying His hunger.

What physical needs do you have at the moment? Do you lack provision? Physical health? Strength to do the work in front of you today? Is your mind discouraged? Is your body weak? While it's imperative that we care for ourselves physically, never divorce this self-care from your communication with the Father. Allow Him to dictate how you go about caring for your body. Let His voice have authority over the cravings and desires that you experience physically. When you're able to say "no" to a physical appetite in order to walk in obedience, you'll be able to deny every ungodly temptation and keep your focus on your Heavenly Father.

APPLICATION QUESTIONS

1) After Jesus' temptation, angels came to minister to Him and restore His strength. We see that His hunger was important, and His need for food was met. Why, then, do you think the gospel writer includes the account of Jesus saying no to Satan's temptation to make bread from stones? Why was it important that Jesus didn't give in to Satan?

2) What physical needs do you have right now that haven't been fully met? What solace can you take from the story of Jesus' physical temptation?

3) How can you care for your body while still ensuring that God has the ultimate authority in your life? How do these go hand in hand? How might your physical desires need to take a backseat to the sovereignty of God?

MAY 14-20

WEEK 20

A JOYFUL GIFT

Then the leaders of fathers' houses made their freewill offerings, as did also the leaders of the tribes, the commanders of thousands and of hundreds, and the officers over the king's work. They gave for the service of the house of God five thousand talents and ten thousand darics of gold, ten thousand talents of silver, eighteen thousand talents of bronze and one hundred thousand talents of iron. And whoever had precious stones gave them to the treasury of the house of the Lord, in the care of Jehiel the Gershonite. Then the people rejoiced because they had given willingly, for with a whole heart they had offered freely to the Lord. David the king also rejoiced greatly.

—1 CHRONICLES 29:6-9 (ESV)

WE'VE ALREADY EXPLORED the concept of giving willingly to God from our finances. But did you know that it can even be *fun*? Here, we see the people of Israel gladly gave of their possessions for the treasury of the Lord. They celebrated their surrender to God, and they also rejoiced "because they had given willingly." Don't miss that. Not only was the gift in itself worth celebrating, but the condition of their hearts was right before the Lord!

It might seem self-centered to rejoice when your heart is right before God; there's a fine line there, to be sure. But there's nothing wrong with thanking God for empowering you to be surrendered to Him! When you find yourself exhibiting godly fruit, and when you start to think and believe what God thinks, it's cause for celebration! James 1:17 tells us that every good thing is a gift from God. Indeed, even our faith is a gift—we can't muster it up on our own. The people of Israel rejoiced because they had been gifted faith—and out of that faith, they'd made a gift of their own back to God.

As you consider ways to have fun, don't forget that communion with God and conformity to His perfect will yields the most lasting enjoyment. Your quality of life will increase when you surrender to Him, even if you face trials and temptations along the way. It may not be an easy life, but as we see here, it's a fulfilling life. Look again at all the riches and luxurious goods that the people gave to the treasury. The Lord had abundantly blessed them! Yet they rejoiced to relinquish these riches to a God whose love and presence was infinitely more valuable. What can you joyfully surrender to God today? How can you thank Him for the faith and trust that He's empowered you to have in Him?

APPLICATION QUESTIONS

1) What's the difference between having grateful joy for your increasing faith and boastfully bragging about how good you are before God? Which were the Israelite people doing in this passage? How can you tell?

2) What riches and blessings has God given you? How can you give them back to Him?

3) How does it change your perspective to realize that God's people rejoiced because of their changed hearts? How has God changed your heart already as you've walked with Him? Take time today to praise Him for making you more like Him!

MAY 21-27

WEEK 21

COSTLY OBEDIENCE

Then Esther sent this reply to Mordecai: "Go, gather together all the Jews who are in Susa, and fast for me. Do not eat or drink for three days, night or day. I and my attendants will fast as you do. When this is done, I will go to the king, even though it is against the law. And if I perish, I perish."

—ESTHER 4:15-16 (NIV)

THIS PASSAGE FROM Esther's story comes after Esther has been kidnapped, forced to join a harem, put through months of cosmetic treatments, separated from her people and her family, and is now facing a lifetime of servitude to a foreign king. Esther receives word that Haman's plot to kill the Jews is about to become a reality. No one in the palace knows that she herself is a Jew. There's one chance to save God's people. She has to go before the king uninvited, a death sentence in that day. Here, Esther's faith costs her something. There's a very real exchange—her safety for God's purpose. Her comfort for the salvation of God's people. This even foreshadows Christ's willingness to die in order that we might be saved from eternal separation from Him!

We enjoy having faith in God when it benefits us: when we are comforted, encouraged, and given a higher purpose in Him. However, many believers struggle to maintain their faith in God when it begins to cost them. Whether faith costs us comfort, friends, jobs, our home, our way of life, or any other number of things—even our lives—it's essential to remember that God's purposes and plans for our lives are ultimately so much better.

It's also important to know that we don't have faith in God for what He can give us. The Christian life doesn't promise to be an easy one; indeed, Jesus said that we will have trouble in this life (John 16:33). So instead of being shocked and offended when God leads us through trials and tests our faith, we should expect to encounter opposition when we live differently from the world.

Esther knew that she might die when she went before the king. But more importantly, she knew that God had a bigger plan in place for His people: that, if she didn't risk her life, the lives of thousands of Jews would be ended—or that God would call someone else to step in and be His hand of salvation. Esther's perspective was wider than the moment she was in.

How about our perspective? Do we see a glimpse of God's bigger picture? Are we willing to sacrifice in faith in order to obey Him? Or are we so committed to our comfort and our way of life that we refuse to step out in faith when it costs us something? If Jesus was willing to give it all in obedience to the Father, how much more should we be willing to do the same!

APPLICATION QUESTIONS

1) Who are some believers you know, or know of, who have sacrificed greatly in order to walk in faith and obedience to God?

2) Why do you think Esther asked her people to join her in prayer and fasting before going in to the king? Who can come alongside you in your faith walk and encourage you?

3) What is God calling you to step into right now in this season of your life? What will this cost you? What will you need to give up in order to obey Him?

MAY 28 – JUNE 3

WEEK 22

A SELFLESS LOYALTY

Then she said, "Behold, your sister-in-law has gone back to her people and her gods; return after your sister-in-law." But Ruth said, "Do not plead with me to leave you or to turn back from following you; for where you go, I will go, and where you sleep, I will sleep. Your people shall be my people, and your God, my God. Where you die, I will die, and there I will be buried. May the Lord do so to me, and worse, if anything but death separates me from you."

—RUTH 1:15-17 (NASB)

TODAY'S CULTURE IS individualistic in nature. It tells us to do what's best for our health, our career, our success, and our well-being. While these things are important, the Bible holds many stories of family loyalty where individuals lay down their own interests for the well-being of those they love. The story of Ruth is one such instance.

Ruth's husband had died, as had the husband of her mother-in-law, Naomi. Orpah, Ruth's sister-in-law, was also a widow. Without their husbands, these three women had to start all over. Naomi thought it best to return to her homeland; she encouraged her daughters-in-law to do the same—to go back to their homeland. Naomi was from the Jewish tribe of Judah, but the two younger women were Moabites, from another people.

Orpah listened to Naomi and returned to her homeland, but Ruth did not. She vowed to stay with her mother-in-law and take care of her. It would have been more convenient, and more in Ruth's self-interest, to start over and make a life for herself in her home country. Instead, she put Naomi's interests above her own. We can learn a lot from her loyalty about what family is meant to look like. When we love others as ourselves, we're able to show compassion, empathy, and steadfast support—even when it doesn't primarily benefit us.

Think about the family unit you're a part of right now. It could be a blood family, a household of roommates, friends, classmates, or simply the community that you're a part of throughout your daily life. Whatever your family looks like, consider how loyalty is a part of your closest relationships. When have others stood by you when it hasn't been easy? When have others put themselves second in order to care for you? How have you shown loyalty and support for others? How can you continue to grow in this area? Ask the Lord this week for help—to show you others through His eyes, and to give you the discernment to meet them where they are and give them what they need.

APPLICATION QUESTIONS

1) How does loyalty play an essential role in keeping a family together?

2) How has disloyalty—or selfishness—kept your family from being as close as it could be?

3) What actions would you like to take to increase the loyalty and service that you show to the members of your family? What actions do you think they could take to better care for you? Ask the Lord to bring your family closer together by increasing the love you have for one another.

JUNE 4-10

WEEK 23

PROVIDING FOR YOUR OWN

> *But if anyone does not provide for his own, and especially for those of his household, he has denied the faith and is worse than an unbeliever.*
>
> —1 TIMOTHY 5:8 (NASB)

HAND IN HAND with loyalty, which we talked about last week, is taking care of one's family. While this verse is directed towards the head of the household, the man of the family, we each have a role to play in taking care of our family. Again, your family may not be comprised of your actual blood relatives, though they are important relationships to cultivate, as well. Whoever God has placed in your life as the closest people to you, are your family.

The principle in 1 Timothy that we see here is a call from Paul to provide for those who are in need, starting with one's household and extending to the church and the local community. The amazing part of this passage is Paul's assertion that lack of care for the people under one's responsibility is evidence of having little faith, or maybe none at all! Why? Because the more one knows God, who is love, the more one will love his brothers and sisters, the orphans and widows, and the needy in one's community.

While we can't be responsible for everyone's well-being, we have a significant role to play in the care of our families and our communities. What are the steps you and your family are taking to care for your tribe? How are you individually providing for and contributing to your family? Maybe you have a job that helps support them financially. Maybe you have a specific set of chores and tasks that are always yours to do. Maybe you have a favorite cause or charity that you contribute to, either in money, time, or resources. Whatever your provision looks like, make sure that you're listening to the Holy Spirit's leading and stepping out in obedience. There may be people in your neighborhood, in your church, or even in your own home that need you. How can you show them God's love in practical ways?

APPLICATION QUESTIONS

1) In your own words, why do you think Paul used such strong words for those who don't provide for their family?

2) Provision can be financial, and financial provision is often the head of the household's responsibility. How else might provision look? How might other members of the household contribute to the family's needs?

3) What groups in your church and your community need to be provided for as well? How can you contribute your time, energy, money, and resources to help one of these groups?

JUNE 11-17

WEEK 24

MY STRENGTH AND MY SONG

Then Moses and the people of Israel sang this song to the Lord, saying, "I will sing to the Lord, for he has triumphed gloriously; the horse and his rider he has thrown into the sea. The Lord is my strength and my song, and he has become my salvation; this is my God, and I will praise him, my father's God, and I will exalt him. The Lord is a man of war; the Lord is his name."

—EXODUS 15:1-3 (ESV)

IN PAST WEEKS, we've talked about the importance of maintaining our physical health. But it would be incomplete to explore the topic of fitness without recognizing that, without God's strength, we can do nothing. In John 15, Jesus tells His disciples that apart from Him, they can do nothing. What was true of the Old Testament nation of Israel in this passage from Exodus is still true for us today: God is our strength. God is our deliverance when we aren't strong enough physically, mentally, or emotionally to overcome what's in front of us. Just as God parted the Red Sea for Moses and His people, He will help us to walk through the trials and tests we face today.

The Israelites worshiped God as the source of their rescue. They didn't say, "We triumphed because Moses was a great leader," or, "We ran so quickly across that dry land that the Egyptians never would have caught us." It's tempting to take credit for the things God has brought us through—especially when we've acted in obedience to what He's told us to do. However, God deserves the glory. He's the deliverer, the all-powerful One. Every ounce of strength we have is ultimately from Him. He allows us to take our next breath, our next step, or our next move.

This week, reflect on the difficult circumstances and seasons of life you've come through. Think about the ways God empowered you to keep going. Think about the situations in which, without Him, you would have given up and been overcome. How has the Lord been your strength and your song? Spend some time this week worshiping and thanking Him for being your strength!

APPLICATION QUESTIONS

1) Why is it tempting to take ultimate credit for the hardships we've overcome in our lives?

2) How can we recognize where we've been obedient and still give God the ultimate glory for our deliverance?

3) What are some hardships and difficulties that God has helped you to overcome? How has He empowered you to keep going and to come out the other side stronger? How has this changed your faith in Him?

JUNE 18-24

WEEK 25

TO FIND SATISFACTION

What do people get for all the toil and anxious striving with which they labor under the sun? All their days their work is grief and pain; even at night their minds do not rest. This too is meaningless. A person can do nothing better than to eat and drink and find satisfaction in their own toil. This too, I see, is from the hand of God, for without him, who can eat or find enjoyment? To the person who pleases him, God gives wisdom, knowledge and happiness, but to the sinner he gives the task of gathering and storing up wealth to hand it over to the one who pleases God. This too is meaningless, a chasing after the wind.

—ECCLESIASTES 2:22-26 (NIV)

SOLOMON'S STATEMENTS IN the above passage may seem contradictory at first. If everything is so meaningless, why enjoy anything? But the author of Ecclesiastes isn't trying to depress us. Instead, he's sharing a key spiritual truth: apart from the Lord, everything we do in life ("under the sun") is futile. We spend decades trying to build our own empires, our own legacies. We work hard so we can buy what we want; we build families and communities. We pour our hearts and minds into creative pursuits. And what comes of it?

According to Solomon, pain, anxiety, and a sense of hopelessness... *without God.* When we work *with* God, however—when everything we do is submitted to Him and ultimately for His glory, what comes of it? We become joyful, wise, knowledgeable, and happy. We find purpose in Him, but not in any of the blessings we acquire. Remember, by themselves, these things don't have inherent, eternal worth. But in Christ, all of our earthly pursuits can have eternal significance.

As you go about your rest and relaxation this week, remember Solomon's words: "A person can do nothing better than to eat and drink and find satisfaction in their own toil." In God, we can enjoy the fruits of our labor. We can kick back, knowing that He will take our ordinary lives and bring eternal, extraordinary things from them. Your week might be mundane, but you can enjoy it nonetheless, because your God watches over and blesses the work of your hands.

What mundane activities take on new significance when seen in this light? How can you be grateful for even the small blessings you enjoy on a day-to-day basis? Don't take the Tuesdays and the Thursdays, the little moments and the repetitive tasks, for granted. They just might be the source of some of your greatest joy.

APPLICATION QUESTIONS

1) According to the passage above, why is it good for man to eat, drink, and enjoy his work?

2) How does God's presence (or lack thereof) in a person's life change the meaning behind everyday tasks and responsibilities?

3) What's something "mundane" in your life that you want to appreciate more? It could be weeknight dinner, a part-time job, or your favorite book at the end of a long day.

JUNE 25–JULY 1

WEEK 26

NO ULTERIOR MOTIVES

But I have trusted and relied on and been confident in Your lovingkindness and faithfulness; My heart shall rejoice and delight in Your salvation. I will sing to the Lord, Because He has dealt bountifully with me.

—PSALM 13:5-6 (AMP)

MANY TIMES, WE trust in God in the hopes of *getting something* from Him. Maybe we trust Him for the blessing of a child, like Abraham and Sarah did. Maybe we trust that He will provide a job, a friend, a spouse, or a new home for us. These dreams and desires are good, but this psalm gives us an example of what it looks like to trust in God's goodness for its own sake.

David was crying out to God in Psalm 13. The first half of the psalm expresses his dejection at God's silence. David had been waiting for an answer, for deliverance, from God. The Lord though, had seemed distant and maybe even absent. David felt abandoned and without assurance of God's faithfulness, his courage faltered.

But the second half of the psalm holds a key truth: David didn't need to see the end result in order to trust in God. He looked back and saw the pattern of God's faithfulness in his life. He knew who he worshiped. God was perfectly good, perfectly faithful, and perfectly loving. David even used three separate phrases to express how secure he was in this truth: "I have trusted and relied on and been confident in Your lovingkindness and faithfulness." David's was a well-founded faith.

And so, while he did ask God for something, David's conviction about God's character was solely based on what God could do for him. Instead, He recognized God for who He is first and foremost. He knew God will never leave him or deal deceitfully with him. Out of this assurance and faith, David left the psalm in a place of hope and faith, ready to face whatever came next. He didn't know exactly what God's plan was, but he knew who God is. And that's all he needed.

This week, challenge yourself in your prayer life. Instead of coming to God primarily with requests, complaints, or worries, come to Him in thankfulness for who He is. Reflect on all the wonderful times He has been faithful in the past. Worship Him simply for being God, for being perfectly holy and good and true. Worship regardless of what He decides to give or provide. You'll find that your heart begins to shift towards the Creator, and away from the created things He gives to you.

APPLICATION QUESTIONS

1) Do you find it natural or easy to worship God without an ulterior motive in mind? Explain your answer.

2) Read Psalm 13 in its entirety. David's tone shifts in verse 5. According to verses 5 and 6, what gives David hope? What does he trust in (hint: it's not necessarily a favorable outcome to his situation)?

3) Spend some time writing a prayer: Thank God for who He is. You may use names or attributes of God found in Scripture. Worship Him without asking for anything, and take note of how this feels different than coming to the Lord primarily with requests.

JULY 2-8

WEEK 27

A NEW FAMILY

> *Jesus said, "Truly, I say to you, there is no one who has left house or brothers or sisters or mother or father or children or lands, for my sake and for the gospel, who will not receive a hundredfold now in this time, houses and brothers and sisters and mothers and children and lands, with persecutions, and in the age to come eternal life."*
>
> —MARK 10:29-30 (ESV)

THIS PASSAGE COMES after the story of the rich young man who asked Jesus how to attain eternal life. The man had kept the Law as well as he could since he was a boy. Jesus tells him, "Go, sell everything you have and give to the poor, and you will have treasure in heaven. Then come, follow me." The Bible tells us that, rather than do what Jesus said, the man went away sad because he was wealthy.

The disciples, processing this encounter and Jesus' following statement ("How hard it is to enter the kingdom of God") asked their Lord, "Who then can be saved?" Jesus replied, "With man this is impossible, but not with God; all things are possible with God."

This is when Peter chimed in: "We have left everything to follow you!" he said. In the disciples' minds, it was still about how much they were giving up. Just like the rich young man, the disciples were fixated on what they were sacrificing to be with Jesus. Jesus, however, shifted their focus to the hundredfold waiting for them in the age to come. The disciples had given up family, acceptance, belonging, and community. They had chosen Jesus over those dearest to them who refused to believe in the truth. Jesus promised that they *were* part of a family: God's family. They would never have to be alone—not truly.

Have you given up relationships or belongings in order to follow God? Have you chosen to obey the Lord rather than to hold onto the things of earth that you treasure? Know that your sacrifice is not in vain. Be comforted by the truth that what Jesus has for you is so much better than anything you give up for His sake. The best gift of all is eternal life—the chance to spend forever with God, as a part of His family. This reward makes every other sacrifice pale in comparison!

APPLICATION QUESTIONS

1) Why do you think the rich young man was willing to follow the Law religiously but not to give up his riches? What does this reveal about the state of his heart?

2) Read Matthew 12:46-50. How does this statement from Jesus pair well with the promise of an eternal family found in Mark 10:29-30?

3) What is something you struggle to surrender to Jesus? Are there any relationships that you've had to let go of in order to follow Him? In contrast, how have you discovered a new family in the kingdom of God?

JULY 9-15

WEEK 28

THE LOVE OF MONEY

Yet true godliness with contentment is itself great wealth. After all, we brought nothing with us when we came into the world, and we can't take anything with us when we leave it. So if we have enough food and clothing, let us be content. But people who long to be rich fall into temptation and are trapped by many foolish and harmful desires that plunge them into ruin and destruction. For the love of money is the root of all kinds of evil. And some people, craving money, have wandered from the true faith and pierced themselves with many sorrows.

—1 TIMOTHY 6:6-10 (NLT)

THE CULTURE OF our world today is saturated with advertisements telling us that we need *more, more, more*. The season's latest fashions, that new furniture set, the most modern make of our favorite car, and so on. It's easy to slip into the longing to be rich that Paul mentioned to Timothy in this passage. Notice that Paul didn't say that *money* is the root of all evil—there are sects of Christianity today that seem to think this is the case, and certain pastors and Christian leaders advocate for getting rid of all your possessions in order to attain a higher level of holiness.

Instead, Paul said that the *love of money* is the root of all kinds of evil. It draws us away from the love of God (see Matthew 6:24) because we drown in the pursuit of *stuff*. The character trait of contentment is one that isn't discussed in church circles as often. It's linked with the fruit of the Spirit, self-control. The more we have control over our urges to consume and to pursue wealth—the more we are content with what God has given us—the more we'll focus on eternal things. We can more fully devote ourselves to advancing the kingdom of God because the purchases and the pursuits we make will be centered around God instead of our own desires.

Is it wrong to buy things? Is it wrong to want possessions? Is it sinful to grow financially? Not at all. But this week, take stock of the heart behind your financial decisions. Are you aiming to create ultimate security for yourself with things and with money? Are you pursuing more, never content, never satisfied with what you have? Are you holding back any part of your finances from the Lord? If the answer to any of these questions is "yes" or even "maybe," take this week to reorient your heart. Thank God for what He's already given you, and ask for His help in stewarding it and making financial decisions. Let every purchase reflect your larger goals. Let every dollar be surrendered to the One who gifted it to you.

After all, only in Him can we be truly content.

APPLICATION QUESTIONS

1) How has culture affected your mindset when it comes to making purchases and financial decisions? Conversely, how are you going against the grain of the culture?

2) Why do you think money is mentioned so often by Jesus? What does this tell us about the potential power of money over our lives?

3) Money isn't evil, but the love of money is. How do you differentiate between the two in your own life? How can you tell if you're beginning to love money more than God?

JULY 16-22

WEEK 29

A GREAT PROJECT

When word came to Sanballat, Tobiah, Geshem the Arab, and the rest of our enemies that I had rebuilt the wall and not a gap was left in it—though up to that time I had not set the doors in the gates—Sanballat and Geshem sent me this message: "Come, let us meet together in one of the villages on the plain of Ono." But they were scheming to harm me; so I sent messengers to them with this reply: "I am carrying on a great project and cannot go down. Why should the work stop while I leave it and go down to you?"

—NEHEMIAH 6:1-3 (NIV)

PART OF BEING FIT, whether physically or otherwise, is discipline. The days when it's hard to get out of bed and work out show us whether we're truly committed to making a change. The workouts that push us to our limits, the setbacks, and challenges, will either drive us to be better or leave us giving up.

Nehemiah was a prophet of God in the Old Testament, and his dedication to rebuilding the wall of Jerusalem after it had been sieged was unshakeable. Though distractions, like his enemies, and challenges surfaced, Nehemiah was fixed on his purpose. He didn't just delegate the work of rebuilding the wall; he himself was on a section of that wall, helping to rebuild it. This is a great example of leadership! We see that not only was Nehemiah physically fit enough to help with the work, but he had the character to follow through alongside his people.

What if we took our overall fitness as seriously as this? What if, when the temptation to compromise, slow down, or give up came, we answered, "I am carrying on a great project and cannot go down." What if we were discerning enough to recognize the things that are designed to harm us, to stop the great work God has for us? In the grand scheme of things, your fitness may not seem that significant, but just imagine if, when God called Nehemiah to do this work, he hadn't been healthy enough to do anything at all? Or what if his commitment was swayed by every smooth-talking enemy and tempting distraction? The wall never would have been rebuilt.

This week, take stock of the things hindering you from staying focused. What are the voices calling at you to give up? What are the things distracting you and holding you back? Conversely, what decisions and commitments do you need to make in order to finish the work? Get specific! Then, enlist the help and accountability of trusted friends to help you stay disciplined to the end.

APPLICATION QUESTIONS

1) What aspects of your fitness do you want to be more committed to? What are some practical steps you can take to make these things priorities in your life?

2) What distractions, naysayers, or temptations are holding you back from staying fully focused on the work God has you doing in the area of your fitness?

3) Who can come alongside you to keep you focused, encouraged, and accountable?

JULY 23-29

WEEK 30

AN ETERNITY OF DELIGHT

On that day the announcement to Jerusalem will be, "Cheer up, Zion! Don't be afraid! For the Lord your God is living among you. He is a mighty savior. He will take delight in you with gladness. With his love, he will calm all your fears. He will rejoice over you with joyful songs."

—ZEPHANIAH 3:16-17 (NLT)

THIS PASSAGE IS incredible when considered in context of the rest of Zephaniah 3. God had just finished telling the prophet Zephaniah that God's people were severely in the wrong. They'd failed to heed God's Word, ignored His warnings, and gone against His law. As a result, judgment was to come upon them for a time.

However, we find this passage nestled into the final verses of the chapter. How? How is this communion and joy and delight possible? It's all due to the forgiving and redemptive nature of God. After Jerusalem's judgment would come a restoration of the relationship between God and His people—an eternal, lasting restoration. God would delight in His people with joy. There would be song and dance and security and love.

What an awesome God we serve—even in the midst of disciplining His people, He looks forward to their restored relationship. Many times, we assume "fun" is only diversion or distraction—shallow entertainment. But here we see a fuller, more lasting definition. Fun is what's left when God's forgiveness and salvation restore us to our Creator once and for all. In Christ Jesus, we are made right with the Father and have an eternity of celebration to look forward to. Not only will we be forgiven—we'll have an endless amount of time to enjoy the presence of our God! What could be more fun than that?

As we glimpse echoes of this paradise in our daily lives on earth, rest assured that no fun we experience today can compare with the amazing future ahead of us. When difficulties come—when the Lord disciplines us with love, when the trials and tests of this world make it hard to believe that something better is coming—remember this promise. In the end, there will be no more temptation, no more separation, no more pain. Only the Lord singing over His redeemed forevermore.

APPLICATION QUESTIONS

1) In your own words, how would you define "fun"?

2) In your walk with God, what role does fun play? How natural is it for you to think of your daily relationship with God as "fun"?

3) What hope and encouragement does it give you to remember that the eternity ahead of us with God is filled with joy and delight and communion with Him?

JULY 30 – AUGUST 5

WEEK 31

CLINGING TO THE LORD

> *[Hezekiah] trusted in the Lord, the God of Israel; and after him there was no one like him among all the kings of Judah, nor among those who came before him. For he clung to the Lord; he did not desist from following Him, but kept His commandments, which the Lord had commanded Moses.*
>
> —2 KINGS 18:5-6 (NASB)

NOTICE WHAT THE author of 2 Kings says made Hezekiah an exceptional king: not his exploits. Not his riches. Not his knowledge. Not his wisdom. Not his abilities. Not his laws or edicts. Not even the connections he had or the people he served.

Hezekiah was an exceptional king because *he clung to the Lord*. Another important thing to note here is the order of the text: Hezekiah followed God, and *then* he was able to keep God's commandments. This is huge. James tells us that faith apart from works is dead, but we don't do works in order to earn our faith. Instead, a heart that has faith in God is empowered by God to obey His word. So Hezekiah clung to the Lord, followed Him and, as a result, was empowered to rule Israel with godliness.

How can this apply to your life this week? Have you been trying to reverse the order of things? Have you put pressure on yourself to be holy and godly without first relying on God Himself? Have you prioritized doing things for God over being with Him? This never works in the long run. Why? Because we don't have the strength to muster up holiness on our own. Only God can truly change our hearts and bring about fruit in our lives.

When it comes down to it, there are very few things that will be remembered about us when we've passed on. Hezekiah's "Greatest Hits" weren't the focus of his legacy. The greatest thing said about him was that he loved the Lord. Let that be the greatest legacy of our lives as well!

APPLICATION QUESTIONS

1) Do you find it easier to do things for God or to spend time being with Him? Explain your answer.

2) Why do you think Christian culture often emphasizes godly action over communion and relationship with God?

3) Read James 1:22-25. In your own words, how are true faith and action linked, according to this passage? Why do they come as a package deal?

AUGUST 6-12

WEEK 32

A NEW FAMILY DYNAMIC

Now his older son was in the field, and as he came and drew near to the house, he heard music and dancing. And he called one of the servants and asked what these things meant. And he said to him, "Your brother has come, and your father has killed the fattened calf, because he has received him back safe and sound." But he was angry and refused to go in. His father came out and entreated him, but he answered his father, "Look, these many years I have served you, and I never disobeyed your command, yet you never gave me a young goat, that I might celebrate with my friends. But when this son of yours came, who has devoured your property with prostitutes, you killed the fattened calf for him!" And he said to him, "Son, you are always with me, and all that is mine is yours. It was fitting to celebrate and be glad, for this your brother was dead, and is alive; he was lost, and is found."

—LUKE 15:25-32 (ESV)

IT'S NO SECRET that family is messy. If you have siblings, in-laws, or even a parent you don't get along with, you'll know this full well. Tempers flare, disagreements happen, jealousy rears its head, and we start comparing ourselves to those we live with and love the most. This is what happened with the older brother in Jesus' Parable of the Prodigal Son.

At this point in the story, the Prodigal Son had left home, squandered his money, realized his mistake, and come home to ask for his father's forgiveness. The older son, his brother, was coming in from a long day of faithful work. He heard the celebration and was indignant. There he was, being good and obedient, and his wayward brother got more of a celebration than he did? It seemed completely unfair. By most standards, he would be right.

But the father of the two sons had a different take on the situation. He told the older brother, "You've been with me all this time. Everything I have is yours." In essence, he was saying, "It's not about who gets the bigger party. The real reward is being a part of my family, having an inheritance from me, being in relationship with me." Instead of comparing the two sons, the father celebrated and cherished them both. More than that, he encouraged them to celebrate and cherish each other.

Godly life isn't just about our relationship with God; it's also about our relationships with our loved ones. On the one hand, this can apply to our church family—the body of believers around the world. But it can also apply to our homes and communities as well: our blood families and our found families. Instead of comparing ourselves to our family members—instead of trying to figure out who's better or who deserves more—what if we learned to champion one another? What if, instead of condemnation, we met those who had been forgiven with joy and celebration? After all, we're all in need of the Father's abundant love and forgiveness.

APPLICATION QUESTIONS

1) Do you find it easy to compare yourself with others, either in your church family or your actual family? Why or why not?

2) Can you relate to the frustration of the older brother in Jesus' parable? What valid points does he have from an earthly perspective?

3) How would it change the atmosphere of your community if your family began to champion one another and celebrate each other's victories?

AUGUST 13-19

WEEK 33

INVESTING IN THE FUTURE

Ship your grain across the sea; after many days you may receive a return. Invest in seven ventures, yes, in eight; you do not know what disaster may come upon the land. . . . As you do not know the path of the wind, or how the body is formed in a mother's womb, so you cannot understand the work of God, the Maker of all things.

—ECCLESIASTES 11:1-2, 5 (NIV)

WE TOUCHED ON this principle of financial stewardship on Week 8, but it's mentioned throughout the Bible: investment. In this passage, Solomon, the author of Ecclesiastes, makes the important point that we can't perfectly predict the future. Investing our money and creating a strong financial foundation for our families is insurance against the economic ups and downs that will inevitably come.

Sometimes, these ups and downs are due to our own circumstances; sometimes, they're the result of the country or community in which we live. Regardless, it's wise to do whatever is in our power to make sure we're responsible with the finances entrusted to us. We also see the principle here that investment in multiple things is wise. After all, putting your eggs into only one basket leaves you liable to more risk than if your investments are spread out.

When it comes down to it, investment is stewardship that looks toward the future. What do you want your children or benefactors to enjoy one day? How do you want to be able to live out your later years? What generosity do you desire to show towards others? Investing demonstrates gratitude to God for the financial blessings He's given to you, and plans ahead for a more rewarding future.

APPLICATION QUESTIONS

1) How do you currently feel about investing your money? Are there any questions or reservations you have about it?

2) What are some of the potential benefits of investing your money in multiple places or ventures?

3) What allowances do you want to make for yourself years from today? What about your family and loved ones?

AUGUST 20-26

WEEK 34

RUN AND NOT GROW WEARY

He gives power to the weak and strength to the powerless. Even youths will become weak and tired, and young men will fall in exhaustion. But those who trust in the Lord will find new strength. They will soar high on wings like eagles. They will run and not grow weary. They will walk and not faint.

—ISAIAH 40:29-31 (NLT)

HOW AMAZING IT is that every breath we draw and every step we take, is empowered by our Heavenly Father! Even when we reach the end of our strength, patience, and understanding, we can rest assured that God has what we need. Have you been trying to do it in your own strength? Have you reached the end of your rope? Are you discouraged and exhausted in any areas of your life this week?

Jesus told those who are weary to come to Him and find rest (Matthew 11:28). You don't have to do life in your own strength, though it's often tempting to try. In fact, this is often the reason we burn ourselves out as believers. We know logically that God offers us peace and rest, but we so rarely lean on Him in the midst of our days and take advantage of that rest. Another important passage on this subject is found in John 15. Jesus tells His disciples right before His crucifixion that they need to abide in Him in order to bear much fruit, and that apart from Him, they can do nothing.

This week, where do you need the Lord's strength? How do you need Him to meet you in your weakness? What rest do you need from Him? Before you turn to people, motivational resources, or other sources of encouragement, spend time with Him and seek His strength.

APPLICATION QUESTIONS

1) What areas of your life currently have you feeling tired or worn out? Why do you think this is?

2) What other sources of strength are you tempted to turn to when you feel exhausted? What benefits do these sources offer?

3) Why is it essential for believers to go to God first and ask for His strength? This can apply to our physical strength, but what other areas of life does it apply to as well?

AUGUST 27 – SEPTEMBER 2

WEEK 35

A CHEERFUL HEART

*A cheerful heart is good medicine, but a
crushed spirit dries up the bones.*
—PROVERBS 17:22 (NIV)

NOT ONLY IS FUN an important spiritual rhythm, it's biologically good for you! Individuals who don't de-stress and take time to do things they enjoy are more susceptible to illnesses. In some cases, they even live shorter lives. That's because our health is holistic; our bodies and our minds are linked. The better health we have mentally, the better our physical health will be, and vice versa.

Many of us lose touch with the activities and habits that help us feel refreshed. Maybe as a child or young person you enjoyed reading, playing a sport, watching a favorite show, or hanging out with friends at a favorite spot. Just because we get older doesn't mean we don't need fun in our routine. How can you rediscover an old hobby, or take up a new one? Are there any recreational activities you've been interested in that you haven't gotten the chance to try?

Additionally, some of the best fun experiences happen with other people. Who can you invite to join you in a class, a meal, or a day trip? Get creative! There's a reason the Bible encourages us to relax and take time off. The more well-rounded we are, the healthier we'll be, and the more Christlike we'll be, too.

Are you struggling with a crushed spirit this week? Are you feeling oppressed by all the responsibilities on your plate? It might seem counterintuitive, but taking time to have fun is actually the key to being more productive in the long run! Brainstorm how you can make time to recharge and do things that replenish your cheerful heart.

APPLICATION QUESTIONS

1) What are some old hobbies or pastimes you can revisit during your downtime?

2) What other things need to be shifted around or eliminated altogether in order to make time for leisure?

3) What are the potential health benefits to making fun more of a priority in your daily and weekly life?

SEPTEMBER 3-9

WEEK 36

WAITING ON GOD

But as for me, I am like a green olive tree in the house of God; I trust in the faithfulness of God forever and ever. I will praise You forever, because You have done it, And I will wait on Your name, for it is good, in the presence of Your godly ones.

—PSALM 52:8-9 (NASB)

TO FULLY UNDERSTAND the significance of David's statements above, it's necessary to look at the rest of the chapter before this point. It goes like this:

> Why do you boast in evil, you mighty man?
> The faithfulness of God endures all day long.
> Your tongue devises destruction,
> Like a sharp razor, you worker of deceit.
> You love evil more than good,
> Lies more than speaking what is right.
> Selah
> You love all words that devour,
> You deceitful tongue.
> But God will break you down forever;
> He will snatch you up and tear you away from your tent,
> And uproot you from the land of the living.
> Selah
> The righteous will see and fear,

And they will laugh at him, saying,
"Behold, the man who would not make God his refuge,
But trusted in the abundance of his riches
And was strong in his evil desire."

Rather than jumping at the chance to grasp worldly security and power, David had waited on the Lord. He knew that any influence, any legacy, that he took hold of in his own power would not last. Only God could make him flourish and keep him sustained.

Are you trusting in the all-powerful God this week to sustain you and direct your paths? In what areas might you be trading faith in Him for faith in other things: power, status, possessions? Wait on God. You'll never regret it and the benefits are eternal—not temporary like the things of earth.

APPLICATION QUESTIONS

1) David faced many adversaries during his life and reign as king—people who wanted to kill him. What do you think these experiences taught him about power, based on Psalm 52?

2) In what areas do you tend to slip into trusting other things besides God for your ultimate fulfillment or security?

3) Why is it significant, in verse 5, that David says God will do the work of dealing with evil people? What does that indicate our role is in our own encounters with evil?

SEPTEMBER 10-16

WEEK 37

FAMILY FEUD

Cain spoke to Abel his brother. And when they were in the field, Cain rose up against his brother Abel and killed him. Then the Lord said to Cain, "Where is Abel your brother?" He said, "I do not know; am I my brother's keeper?"

—GENESIS 4:8-9 (ESV)

WE ALL HAVE that one family member that we just don't get along with. Maybe our personalities rub each other the wrong way or maybe there's a history full of pain and conflict. Maybe there's just something we can't put our finger on that keeps us from enjoying that person's company. As uncomfortable as family get-togethers can be, few families deal with the level of animosity and hatred that Cain had for his brother, Abel.

But why so much ill will? Genesis tells us that Abel's sacrifice, which was the best of his crops, was pleasing to God, while Cain's sacrifice—an unspecified selection from his flocks and herds—wasn't accepted by God. Was it jealousy that drove Cain to hate his brother then? Maybe. Or was it insecurity about his place before God? We'll never know for sure, but the Bible is clear that Cain was angry and his face was downcast or gloomy.

So many times, our own issues cloud our relationships with others. Cain didn't truly have anything to be angry at Abel for; his issue was between himself and God. It's remarkable how many family conflicts are a result of the inner insecurities, hurts, and baggage that we carry around. This week, reflect on any relationships in your family that are less healthy than you'd like them to be. It's so easy to focus on what the other person could do better, but what about yourself? How can you reach out to mend the relationship? What sins do you need to confess and repent of? What inner issues do you and God need to address before you see this person again?

While some family conflicts are not our fault, there's always a level of power we have: the power to give the situation to God, take responsibility for our own selves, and make sure that we're being as loving and wise as possible. Cain chose not to address his own hurts and bitterness and the consequences were deadly.

APPLICATION QUESTIONS

1) What relationships in your family are broken or injured? Why do you think this is?

2) What is your responsibility in these relationships? What is not your responsibility/what can you not control?

3) What internal fears, bitterness, or other issues do you need to work on with the Lord in order to be a better family member?

SEPTEMBER 17-23

WEEK 38

A DEN OF ROBBERS

Jesus entered the temple courts and drove out all who were buying and selling there. He overturned the tables of the money changers and the benches of those selling doves. "It is written," he said to them, "'My house will be called a house of prayer,' but you are making it 'a den of robbers.'"

—MATTHEW 21:12-13 (NIV)

JUST AS WE'VE discussed godly principles of money management, we see the flip side in this passage. There's a wrong way to steward money. There are ways to anger God with the way we use what we have. The issue here wasn't that people were buying or selling. It wasn't even that they were buying and selling sacrifices—that had long been a practice in Israel.

The issue was that the vendors who sold the doves and the moneychangers who made currency exchanges were doing so with the wrong heart. Their rates were inflated, taking advantage of their patrons. They weren't doing business honestly and they'd allowed their business to enter the temple, which was a space for honoring the Lord. The hypocrisy in this angered and grieved Jesus. These people had forsaken worship of God in order to worship their own money.

Maybe some of us have done the same. Again, we're not saying God doesn't want to be a part of your work, your income, your provision—but He does want to take precedence *over* it. The day we lose sight of what comes first is the day we begin to worship money. And, as we talked about in a previous week, God makes it clear that we can't serve both God and money (Matthew 6:24). Jesus could see beyond the moneychangers' and vendors' activities to their hearts. They were more interested in profit than in meeting with and serving Him—and they were leading others to do the same. As much as we tend to think the way we use our money stops with us, we're subtly passing along a legacy of financial stewardship. Whether it's to our kids, those we mentor, or simply the watching world, we are creating a financial culture with every decision we make.

What does your spending and earning say about your heart? Does God have precedence—does He come first—or will you trade time and intimacy with Him in order to make a little more money? It's convicting to realize when our allegiance has begun to slip, but just as Jesus cleansed the temple, God wants to cleanse our hearts—we are the temple of the Holy Spirit. Ask Him to reveal any places in your life where money has begun to supersede Him, and surrender to the changes He wants to make!

APPLICATION QUESTIONS

1) What "good excuses" might the moneychangers and vendors have had for conducting their business inside the temple (for example: traveling Jews who came to the temple often didn't bring sacrifices with them, so there was a need for someone to provide these animals)?

2) What "good excuses" might we have for the instances in our lives when money takes precedence over God (for example, we have to provide for our family)?

3) What does dependence on money over God ultimately reveal about our faith? What are we really believing about God when we can't trust Him to provide for us?

SEPTEMBER 24-30

WEEK 39

RUNNING WITH ENDURANCE

Therefore, since we also have such a great cloud of witnesses surrounding us, let's rid ourselves of every obstacle and the sin which so easily entangles us, and let's run with endurance the race that is set before us, looking only at Jesus, the originator and perfecter of the faith, who for the joy set before Him endured the cross, despising the shame, and has sat down at the right hand of the throne of God.

—HEBREWS 12:1-2 (NASB)

ONE OF THE SKILLS a runner works on is endurance. If you're running any distance longer than a few hundred meters, your body has to work up the strength to sustain a fast run over a period of time. For instance, someone who's running a mile or two-mile race may put in five to ten miles a day in order to build up endurance. That way, when race day arrives, they're not just prepared to cover the distance but to do so with excellence and leftover energy.

The same is true in our "race" with Christ. Here, the author of Hebrews, who has just finished retelling the stories of the saints of old, tells his audience to look to Jesus for strength. The Christian life isn't easy—a topic we've already talked about in past weeks. But how do we excel in this run? How do we keep going when our lungs are burning and our muscles are weak?

One of the best things we can do to increase our endurance is to get rid of dead weight. Here, that weight is identified as sin. Sin holds us back, entangles us, and slows us down. Sin takes our energy and leaves us distracted and discouraged. If we're going to keep our eyes on the finish line—on Jesus—sin has to go.

Who is our ultimate example in this race of faith? Jesus Christ Himself. Though He never sinned, He still endured a difficult earthly life, took on our sin at the cross, and kept going despite the most excruciating torture and death. He spent thirty-three years training and preparing, kept His eyes on the Father, and stayed strong. He didn't stop running, didn't stop trusting, and didn't stop pursuing God's purpose for His life.

What's holding you back? What training regimen does God have you in, even now? Do you need more practice in order to build up strength and endurance? Try looking at the spiritual tests and opportunities in your life from this perspective. How might the steps you're taking today prepare you for what He has in store for you down the road? When all else fails and your strength seems gone, look to Jesus. Because of His finished work, you have everything you need to take the next step.

APPLICATION QUESTIONS

1) Most of us have seen Olympic races. What uncelebrated, unseen work goes into these athletes' successes? How many hours do you think they've trained to get to races that last only a few seconds or minutes?

2) Do you tend to look at spiritual tests and hardships only for what they are in the moment, or can you look ahead and see the long-term benefits of being trained by them?

3) What's one sin that's currently holding you back from being as free and fast as you can be? How does wrestling with this sin keep you from looking to Jesus Christ?

OCTOBER 1-7

WEEK 40

UNSHAKEABLE JOY

"Truly, truly, I say to you, you will weep and lament, but the world will rejoice. You will be sorrowful, but your sorrow will turn into joy. When a woman is giving birth, she has sorrow because her hour has come, but when she has delivered the baby, she no longer remembers the anguish, for joy that a human being has been born into the world. So also you have sorrow now, but I will see you again, and your hearts will rejoice, and no one will take your joy from you."

—JOHN 16:20-22 (ESV)

JESUS SPOKE THESE words to His disciples in the garden of Gethsemane, only a few hours before He was tortured and crucified. He was warning them about His impending departure, but promising that a greater future lay ahead: a future where they would never have to be apart from Him again.

Of all the things that bring us delight, joy, and celebration, the presence of God should be the first. While we enjoy every good gift that God gives to us (James 1:17), it's essential to remember the ultimate prize: knowing and being with God Himself. The disciples had left everything behind to follow Jesus, and now He had to leave them. This is why His encouragement and reassurance to them was so important. Jesus likened it to the labor and delivery pain that a woman endures to bring her child into the world. In the moment, there's immense suffering; afterwards, it's all worth it because of the result.

Jesus knew His disciples would face incredible opposition in the years following that night. All but one of them would be martyred for their faith. They'd endure ridicule, rejection, torture, and death. They'd have to do so without Jesus' physical presence beside them, as they'd enjoyed for the previous three years. Yet despite all this hardship, Jesus encouraged them to know that, in the future, their sorrow would be transformed into joy. They'd be in His presence forever.

No matter what hardships you might be facing this week, or how your walk with God might be difficult, know that there's a better reality coming. There's an eternal future for you as a child of God that will be the most joyful, celebratory, fulfilling existence possible. Now, we see as in a mirror dimly (1 Corinthians 13:12), but when we're face-to-face with Jesus, nothing will be able to take away our joy. And that's worth everything that happens in between!

APPLICATION QUESTIONS

1) How do you think the disciples felt listening to their Savior's words that night in the garden? What questions do you think they might have had?

2) Why did Jesus know His followers needed the promise of the eternity that lay before them? How would that reassurance bolster their faith in the days and years to come?

3) Paul alludes to the same allegory of childbirth in Romans 8:22: "For we know that the whole creation has been groaning together in the pains of childbirth until now." How have you seen your world "groaning" as it awaits the new heaven and new earth that will come when Christ returns?

OCTOBER 8-14

WEEK 41

A GRACIOUS AND COMPASSIONATE GOD

But to Jonah this seemed very wrong, and he became angry. He prayed to the Lord, "Isn't this what I said, Lord, when I was still at home? That is what I tried to forestall by fleeing to Tarshish. I knew that you are a gracious and compassionate God, slow to anger and abounding in love, a God who relents from sending calamity. Now, Lord, take away my life, for it is better for me to die than to live." But the Lord replied, "Is it right for you to be angry?"

—JONAH 4:1-4 (NIV)

WHAT AN INTERESTING response to salvation from one of God's prophets! Jonah's entire role as a prophet was to speak God's words to the people, to warn them to repent. But when the citizens of Nineveh, one of the most wicked cities on earth listened . . . Jonah was furious. This man, whom God had just shown forgiveness, refused to forgive others.

Isn't this so like us today? We want to take advantage of all the grace and mercy God has to offer us, but so quickly we judge and condemn others. It's as if we think some are worthy of grace and others aren't. But the Bible tells a different story. Isaiah 53:2-3 says this: "God looks down from heaven on all mankind to see if there are any who understand, any who seek God. Everyone has turned away, all have become corrupt; there is no one who does good, not even one."

The truth is clear. Without God drawing us to Himself, without His salvation and mercy, none of us would seek Him out. None of us would be good enough to deserve eternity with Him. What Jonah was forgetting was that even he hadn't been worthy of God's love. It didn't matter how wicked the Ninevites were—Jonah and the Ninevites were on the same playing field spiritually: both desperately in need of salvation.

When we remember that God is the only truly holy One, we have more grace and mercy for others. Why? Because we truly understand the grace and mercy that have been shown to us. This is something even Jonah acknowledged. He said, "I knew that you are a gracious and compassionate God, slow to anger and abounding in love, a God who relents from sending calamity." While he was all too happy to experience God's compassion for himself, he didn't want anyone else to turn from their sin and experience it.

Let's not allow our hearts to get to this place. Let's stay humble before the Lord. Let's always remember the order: God pursued us. God purchased our salvation. We did nothing to deserve it. And as we come to remember that He is the One worthy of worship and thanks, we'll begin to see others with the same grace and compassion that we have received from Him.

APPLICATION QUESTIONS

1) Can you relate to Jonah's sense of self-righteousness? Explain your answer.

2) Jonah knew God well enough to see the Ninevites' salvation coming, even before he obeyed God. Is there anyone you've hesitated to share the good news with? What do you think is holding you back? Is it the same thing as Jonah, or something different?

3) How does the knowledge that God did all the work of salvation take pressure off of you and me?

OCTOBER 15-21

WEEK 42

SIBLING LOYALTY

> *When the cloud removed from over the tent, behold, Miriam was leprous, like snow. And Aaron turned toward Miriam, and behold, she was leprous. And Aaron said to Moses, "Oh, my lord, do not punish us because we have done foolishly and have sinned. Let her not be as one dead, whose flesh is half eaten away when he comes out of his mother's womb." And Moses cried to the Lord, "O God, please heal her—please."*
>
> —NUMBERS 12:10-13 (ESV)

MIRIAM WAS PUNISHED by God for not trusting in His words to her, Moses, and Aaron. The leprosy with which God struck her was a vicious disease. It meant social isolation, physical deterioration, and a lack of sensation and feeling that meant certain danger and injury.

It would have been understandable in this moment for Miriam's brothers, Aaron and Moses, to jump on her too. "What were you thinking?" they could have demanded. "You know better than to doubt God! You deserve what you got." Instead, we see a different response. Aaron pleads with Moses, the go-between for Israel and God, to pray for their sister. Moses needed no other prompting—his heart was filled with compassion as well.

Here we see two brothers emulating an extremely important family quality—loyalty. Though their sister was in the wrong, they made intercession for her. They forgave her. They were humble enough to realize that they'd both made mistakes before too. And they came to God as the solution to their family's need for healing.

What if more families today did just this? What if we forgave one another? What if we saw past our self-righteousness or our need to be right? What if we were loyal even when family members failed us or fell short of our expectations? What if we were humble enough to come before God and intercede for those we love? Is it always easy? Of course not. But what is family if not loyal to one another?

God is the ultimate example of familial loyalty. Again and again throughout Scripture, we see Him protect, forgive, and give strength to His chosen children. Even when they mess up, sin, turn their backs on Him, and blatantly disobey His Word, He still has mercy. He sends Jesus Christ, the perfect sacrifice, to create a way for His family to be restored. How amazing is God's faithfulness to His people!

As we strive to build healthy, whole families, let's look to God's example and love our own with the same love He's given to us. Who can you intercede for in your family this week?

APPLICATION QUESTIONS

1) Miriam had sinned against God with her unbelief, but her two brothers prayed on her behalf, and her leprosy was healed by God. Why do you think God allowed Moses and Aaron the opportunity to pray for their sister?

2) In your opinion, what keeps family members from being as loyal to one another as they could be? Are there cultural influences at play? Is loyalty affected by circumstances or family history?

3) What might it cost you to be loyal to those in your family—what might you need to give up?

OCTOBER 22-28

WEEK 43

BLOOD MONEY

Then Haman said to King Ahasuerus, "There is a certain people scattered and dispersed among the peoples in all the provinces of your kingdom; their laws are different from those of all other people and they do not comply with the king's laws, so it is not in the king's interest to let them remain. If it is pleasing to the king, let it be decreed that they be eliminated, and I will pay ten thousand talents of silver into the hands of those who carry out the king's business, to put into the king's treasuries."

—ESTHER 3:8-9 (NASB)

JUST AS MONEY can be a channel through which we glorify God, money can be a motivator of evil. In the story of Esther, part of Haman's proposal to the king to kill all the Jews was a hefty sum. In a way, Haman bribed the king, and the king took these funds in exchange for murdering God's people.

The dangers of greed are many—we've touched on a few of them already in past weeks. But here, we see a clear result of one of the worst kinds of financial exchanges: blood money. Judas came along years later as another example of this; he accepted thirty pieces of silver in exchange for turning in Jesus to the authorities to be crucified.

Are these exchanges *really* about the money? We may never know without seeing the hearts of those involved, but Proverbs 1:18-19 (ESV) says this about men who rush to do evil: "These men lie in wait for their own blood; they set an ambush for their own lives. Such are the ways of everyone who is greedy for unjust gain; it takes away the life of its possessors." We see this truth played out both in the story of Haman and the story of Judas; both die as a result of their betrayal of God's people—one from sentencing, the other from guilt and regret.

Now, this may not even remotely apply to many of us directly, but there's still a financial principle to be grasped here. Money can be an indication of your heart. Matthew 6:21 (NIV) says, "Where your treasure is, there your heart will be also." What are we willing to trade for a few more dollars? What are we willing to abandon? Who are we willing to betray? We like to think that our bank statements don't matter much in the long run, but you can tell a lot about someone by the way they spend.

It's likely you'll never commit a financial crime, but is your money betraying your intimacy with God in any way? Are there any areas of life in which you've allowed the direction of your spending to shift from glorifying God to working against His ways and His purposes? Take this week to search your accounts, and your heart, to evaluate these questions.

APPLICATION QUESTIONS

1) Why do you think the king (in Haman's story) and the religious elite (in Judas' story) accepted bribe money for crimes in the first place? What does this tell us about their hearts?

2) Where is your treasure currently—what things dominate your thoughts, your days, and your dollars? Is there anything that has a stronger hold on you than you'd like?

3) What's the next step you need to take in managing your finances in order to glorify the Lord with your money?

OCTOBER 29 – NOVEMBER 4

WEEK 44

GOING AGAINST THE GRAIN

Daniel then said to the guard whom the chief official had appointed over Daniel, Hananiah, Mishael and Azariah, "Please test your servants for ten days: Give us nothing but vegetables to eat and water to drink. Then compare our appearance with that of the young men who eat the royal food, and treat your servants in accordance with what you see." So he agreed to this and tested them for ten days. At the end of the ten days they looked healthier and better nourished than any of the young men who ate the royal food. So the guard took away their choice food and the wine they were to drink and gave them vegetables instead.

—DANIEL 1:11-16 (NIV)

THROUGHOUT GOD'S WORD, we see His children place their faith in Him over and over again. This, however, is one of the unique instances in which this faith had a directly physical result. Daniel and his friends were Israelite exiles, enslaved by Babylon, and taken away from their homeland. Part of Babylon's indoctrination process was recruiting the "best and the brightest" from Israel's next generation to come to the palace and be trained, educated, and employed by the king.

Why Daniel's refusal to eat the royal food? Partially because some of the ingredients were strictly forbidden by the Law, such as pork. But it was also because Daniel had more faith in God's ability to sustain him than in the riches and the trappings of the Babylonian court. Instead of trying to be an instigator, Daniel's heart was to remain faithful to his God, even if it cost him social status.

This is an important principle to remember as we continue to grow in our journey of fitness. Instead of capitulating to the latest cultural fads, customs, or fitness strategies, we need to be wise about what we're putting into our bodies and how we're stewarding them. Now, this could be different for everyone—after all, many of the young exiles who came to the palace had no qualms about eating the rich food. Daniel wasn't worried about convincing everyone else to do what he did; he simply followed his personal convictions.

Think about your fitness journey. Whether it's exercise, diet, lifestyle, or all of these, what are the areas in which you've placed more trust in human strategy than in God's ability to sustain and grow you? There's nothing wrong with doing research and trying different approaches, but at the end of the day, where is your ultimate confidence? Do you think that you *need* someone else's strategies to live a healthy, wholesome life? Or do you know that it's God who sustains you, and who will lead you to the right routines and rhythms for you personally?

Have faith in God, not only in physical fitness—you'll find that both your relationship with Him and your health improve.

APPLICATION QUESTIONS

1) What's one aspect of the physical fitness world today that has benefitted you personally? What's one cultural fitness trend that you see as problematic?

2) Do you tend to put your ultimate faith in others' abilities to keep you healthy? Or do you simply use the strategies and science available to you as tools? Explain your answer.

3) What do you think made it tempting for Daniel to give in and do what every other exile in Babylon was doing? What may have made it easier to stick to his convictions?

NOVEMBER 5-11

WEEK 45

MANDATORY R&R

Then Moses said, "Eat it today, for today is a Sabbath to the Lord; today you will not find it in the field. Six days you shall gather it, but on the seventh day, the Sabbath, there will be none." Yet it came about on the seventh day that some of the people went out to gather, but they found none. Then the Lord said to Moses, "How long do you refuse to keep My commandments and My instructions? See, the Lord has given you the Sabbath; for that reason He gives you bread for two days on the sixth day. Remain, everyone, in his place; no one is to leave his place on the seventh day." So the people rested on the seventh day.

—EXODUS 16:25-30 (NASB)

A LITTLE BACKSTORY to preface this passage. . . . Before this point, God had established the Sabbath as a nonnegotiable commandment for His people. One day per week, they were to stop their work and observe a day of rest. This was also the day that the Israelites would often go to worship corporately and hear from the Word of God. The problem was that over time, the people had neglected to observe this day. The temptation to keep working, gathering, and providing for themselves was too great; instead of trusting Him to provide, they took matters into their own hands.

This is where we pick up the story. The Israelites were gathering manna, the bread from heaven that God provided in the wilderness outside of the Promised Land. Moses instructed the people to get two days' worth of food on the day before the

Sabbath. Did they listen? Of course not. That would require confidence in God's ability to keep the manna from spoiling and to sustain them. How easily we rely on our own abilities to provide for ourselves and forget all the provision God has given us in the past! This is what happened in this passage.

Finally, when God reprimands them through Moses, they listen and understand the meaning behind the Sabbath. As Jesus would later tell the Pharisees and religious officials, the Sabbath was made for man, not the other way around (Mark 2:27)—meaning that the moment it becomes more about observing rules and being pious than about resting and communing with the Father is the moment we lose the heart behind the commandment.

How often do we neglect to rest and reset, finding space to commune with God? In our world, stimuli and distractions are only a few taps away, available 24/7. Is there even such a thing as true rest any more? To find it, we'll need to set aside our confidence in our own abilities. Resting requires trust in God to provide where we can't, to sustain us even when we're not working, and to take care of us beyond what we can do ourselves. It also prepares our hearts to hear clearly from Him, removing all the noise that would make this more difficult.

The time you take to rest is somewhat indicative of your confidence in God's provision. So allow yourself a day this week to step back and leave things in His hands. He is fully capable of taking care of it while you reset.

APPLICATION QUESTIONS

1) Do you find it easy or difficult to take time to rest? Why do you think this is?

2) What aspects of our culture today make it difficult to truly rest?

3) What benefits do we forfeit when we neglect to spend time resting and in communion with the Lord? How does this affect our overall well-being in the long run?

NOVEMBER 12-18

WEEK 46

THE ORIGINAL 300

The Lord said to Gideon, "The people with you are too many for me to give the Midianites into their hand, lest Israel boast over me, saying, 'My own hand has saved me.' Now therefore proclaim in the ears of the people, saying, 'Whoever is fearful and trembling, let him return home and hurry away from Mount Gilead.'" Then twenty-two thousand of the people returned, and ten thousand remained. And the Lord said to Gideon, "The people are still too many. Take them down to the water, and I will test them for you there, and anyone of whom I say to you, 'This one shall go with you,' shall go with you, and anyone of whom I say to you, 'This one shall not go with you,' shall not go."

—JUDGES 7:2-4 (ESV)

THE ISRAELITES WERE about to face a formidable enemy army and they had the numbers to match them. This was a problem, however, because it offered the potential for God's people to take full credit for their impending victory, instead of crediting God with the win. For this reason, God knew that He had to decrease their numbers in order to increase His glory. He instructed Gideon, the leader of the forces, to cut down the army's numbers multiple times.

In the end, God ended up using a mere three hundred Israelite men against an immense opposition force. The odds were stacked highly in the enemy's favor—and that's just how God wanted it. When the battle was over, no one on the Israelites' side could take credit for the victory. Instead, they worshiped God and gave Him all the glory.

GET CLOSER

Sometimes in life, it feels like the odds are stacked against us. We don't think we have what it takes to fulfill the promises God has spoken over our lives. We see our flaws, inadequacies, weaknesses, and the odds against us seem insurmountable in comparison. But if we focus more on the Lord and less on our own shortcomings, the potential for faith is immense. In our weakness, God has the ability to show Himself strong (2 Corinthians 12:9). God may just be setting you up for an opportunity to glorify Him! What an amazing privilege to be a conduit for His glory. Think of the people who might come to know and worship Him through your testimony.

Instead of fixating on the odds, fix your mind and your heart on God. What is He developing in you during this season? He wants a heart of faith in Him more than He wants you to be successful or skilled or impressive. The goal of the Christian walk isn't to be Jesus Himself, but to become like Him as we trust in His power. We can't do it in our own strength—and that's exactly the point.

How is God bringing Himself glory through your weakness today?

APPLICATION QUESTIONS

1) What do you think the 300 Israelite soldiers were thinking as they watched their ranks decrease and shrink again and again?

2) What weaknesses or shortcomings are you all too aware of in yourself? What things make it difficult to have confidence in God's ability to bring about victory in your life?

3) What might it look like practically to shift your focus from your own shortcomings to God's strength? How might this affect how you go about your daily life?

NOVEMBER 19-25

WEEK 47

RADICAL FORGIVENESS

Then Joseph said to his brothers, "I am Joseph; does my father still live?" But his brothers could not answer him, for they were dismayed in his presence. And Joseph said to his brothers, "Please come near to me." So they came near. Then he said: "I am Joseph your brother, whom you sold into Egypt. But now, do not therefore be grieved or angry with yourselves because you sold me here; for God sent me before you to preserve life."
—GENESIS 45:3-5 (NKJV)

IN THE FAMILY portions of our study, we've looked again and again at the concept of forgiveness: extending the grace with which we ourselves have been blessed by God. Joseph's story is one of the most poignant biblical examples of familial grace. Joseph's brothers had hated him, ridiculed him, attacked him, sold him, and left him for dead. They'd shown no remorse for their actions, yet here they were, unknowingly asking this same little brother for food. They were desperate—there was a famine in the land. If Joseph were going to exact his revenge, this was the perfect opportunity to do so. They were totally at his mercy.

Instead, decades after the events that had catapulted Joseph into second-in-command of Egypt, he stood before his brothers and forgave them. Instead of focusing on the wrongs that had been done long before, Joseph chose to focus on the good God had brought out of the difficulties that he'd faced (Romans 8:28).

His brothers, likewise, had been humbled and matured by time. They were wise enough to know their mistakes and to ask forgiveness, yielding to the vision and purpose Joseph had seen in his dream so many years before. In repentance, they bowed with respect before their brother.

Do we have the same maturity that Joseph had—to look at the good and the bad and give God glory for His plans coming to pass? Or do we fixate on the wrongs that have been done to us, harbor bitterness and unforgiveness in our hearts, and hold grudges against those closest to us? The more time we spend ruminating on the past, the less time we have to step into what God has called us to today. Of course, familial conflicts and issues need to be addressed, but if we allow hurts and bitterness to consume us and we refuse to forgive, we'll never be free to move forward.

God commands us to love and forgive others, just as we have been loved and forgiven (Ephesians 4:31-32). Whom do you need to forgive? What wrongs do you need to examine, address, and let go of? Where do you need help moving forward? Sometimes, this is a long process and can require help from others. Other times, other wrongs may only take a few moments to release into the waiting hands of the Lord. There is freedom in forgiveness. Again, this isn't to say that certain relationships aren't unhealthy and even unsafe, but the part you have control over is what you choose to do in your heart. Will you forgive as you have been forgiven?

APPLICATION QUESTIONS

1) In your own words, what's the difference between forgiveness and reconciliation? Are both always possible? Explain.

2) What hurts or wrongs are you currently struggling to forgive and move on from? What makes these things so difficult to let go of, do you think?

3) Because Jesus, who had every right to harbor unforgiveness towards those who wronged Him, forgave us, we now have the power to obey His commandment and forgive others. Take some time to pray about anyone you haven't forgiven and ask for God's strength in letting go and extending grace towards these individuals. (Remember to operate wisely and safely in your relationships with those who have hurt you over and over again.)

NOVEMBER 26–DECEMBER 2

WEEK 48

NON-MONEY GIFTS

Then the whole Israelite community withdrew from Moses' presence, and everyone who was willing and whose heart moved them came and brought an offering to the Lord for the work on the tent of meeting, for all its service, and for the sacred garments. All who were willing, men and women alike, came and brought gold jewelry of all kinds: brooches, earrings, rings and ornaments. They all presented their gold as a wave offering to the Lord. Everyone who had blue, purple or scarlet yarn or fine linen, or goat hair, ram skins dyed red or the other durable leather brought them. Those presenting an offering of silver or bronze brought it as an offering to the Lord, and everyone who had acacia wood for any part of the work brought it. Every skilled woman spun with her hands and brought what she had spun—blue, purple or scarlet yarn or fine linen. And all the women who were willing and had the skill spun the goat hair. The leaders brought onyx stones and other gems to be mounted on the ephod and breast piece. They also brought spices and olive oil for the light and for the anointing oil and for the fragrant incense. All the Israelite men and women who were willing brought to the Lord freewill offerings for all the work the Lord through Moses had commanded them to do.

—EXODUS 35:20-29 (NIV)

UNTIL THIS POINT, we've looked at finances literally—giving money as an act of worship to God. But part of financial generosity and financial worship is using the materials and skills God has gifted to you. Whether you're utilizing your resources to make money or, as in this passage, to serve the house of the Lord, it's essential to surrender everything we have to God.

What talents, skills, and passions do you have? What has God placed inside of you that can help advance and serve His kingdom? Do you love to create? Are you an excellent organizer or bookkeeper? What resources, aside from money, do you have at your disposal? Do you have a place to host others? A car to offer rides? Things you don't need any more that could be sold or donated to help others?

Once you begin to think about the possibilities, it's inspiring to consider the difference your resources could make for someone else. Maybe you can even teach a skill that helps someone else make a living, provide for their family, or enjoy themselves. There are so many possibilities for what your gift can do.

This week, think outside the box—past writing a check or swiping your card. What contribution can you give to your church and your community? What skills and resources can you utilize for a greater kingdom impact? Pray through these questions and write down anything God impresses upon your heart. Seek out others for confirmation, too—they might see your skills and resources even more clearly than you do!

APPLICATION QUESTIONS

1) What non-monetary offerings do you have to give? What unique skills, talents, or resources has God blessed you with?

2) How might the things you listed above be utilized to further the kingdom of God?

3) Who knows you well enough to speak into what you have to offer? Whom do you know well enough to encourage with this same insight?

DECEMBER 3-9

WEEK 49

THE LAMP OF THE BODY

The eye is the lamp of the body. So, if your eye is healthy, your whole body will be full of light, but if your eye is bad, your whole body will be full of darkness. If then the light in you is darkness, how great is the darkness!
—MATTHEW 6:22-23 (ESV)

THIS IS AN important aspect of wholeness and health—our minds. Just as the body's health is directly affected by what we put into it, our minds and hearts are affected by what we feed them. What we take in with our senses can be healthy and good for us, or it can be damaging and counterproductive to the life God wants us to have.

Think about the abundance of content out there today; we have access to more information, entertainment, and raw material than any generation to date. A few typed words and clicks can get you access to virtually anything you want to find, learn, or watch. This comes with a great responsibility. If you're a parent, you know how difficult it is to monitor what your kids take in. But what about you? What "filters" are you placing on your eyes and ears? What things aren't allowed to enter? What parameters do you use to decide what to fill your mind with?

Everything's connected—everything contributes to your overall fitness. You can be physically in shape, but if you're filling your head with junk, you're still not totally healthy. It will also affect your relationship with God. This week, prayerfully think through the content you take in. Study God's Word and make a list of themes, words, or other characteristics that you do *not* want to continue filling your mind and heart with. Then, identify the things you're currently taking in that meet these criteria. Start practically. Commit to giving up these things for seven days, or thirty days, or even a year. Find someone who can keep you accountable to this conviction.

You'll begin to notice a difference in the way you think, talk, and act. Things that were second nature will become less so because you're not taking in that content any longer. This applies not only to earthly things but also to spiritual things: Are you filling yourself with the truth of God's Word? Are you focusing on what's true, good, and beautiful (Philippians 4:8)? There's immense power in what you choose to fill your mind and heart with—don't squander that power.

APPLICATION QUESTIONS

1) As you pray through this week's content, what are some of the things you want to cut out of your "diet" in this area? What makes this difficult for you to consider?

2) Who is someone that can walk alongside you in this commitment and keep you accountable when you're tempted to compromise?

3) You can empty your mind of unhealthy things, but it won't thrive until you fill it with life-giving things. What are some of the "replacements" you want to start taking in more of on a daily basis?

DECEMBER 10-16

WEEK 50

A LITTLE TOO MUCH FUN

Now when the people saw that Moses delayed to come down from the mountain, the people assembled around Aaron and said to him, "Come, make us a god who will go before us; for this Moses, the man who brought us up from the land of Egypt—we do not know what happened to him." Aaron said to them, "Tear off the gold rings which are in the ears of your wives, your sons, and your daughters, and bring them to me." So all the people tore off the gold rings which were in their ears and brought them to Aaron. Then he took the gold from their hands, and fashioned it with an engraving tool and made it into a cast metal calf; and they said, "This is your god, Israel, who brought you up from the land of Egypt." Now when Aaron saw this, he built an altar in front of it; and Aaron made a proclamation and said, "Tomorrow shall be a feast to the Lord." So the next day they got up early and offered burnt offerings, and brought peace offerings; and the people sat down to eat and to drink, and got up to engage in lewd behavior.

—EXODUS 32:1-6 (NASB)

MOSES HAD BEEN on the mountain for several weeks when the Israelites lost patience with their leader. He had gone to hear from the Lord and the people had sent him because they were too scared and unwilling to hear from God themselves. Eventually, they started to get restless. What had happened to Moses? Had he died? Had he abandoned them to hang out with God indefinitely?

Aaron was, for all intents and purposes, second in charge at this point. The people went to him and requested that he construct a god for them from gold they had on hand. On the surface, this seems ludicrous, but how often do we get tired of waiting for a word from God and try to replace the silence with our own "gods"? The party these Israelites threw was probably a great time—the dancing and other festivities indicate they were having fun. But they'd allowed their distraction and recreation to become sinful. There were no boundaries for them—they'd committed blasphemy, trying to define God (and His rules) for themselves.

Fun is an essential part of life, but left unchecked, it can lead to places we never intended to go—consequences we never saw coming. It can literally destroy lives (after this, many of the people were killed as punishment for their sin). Things done "in good fun" have hurt families, destroyed marriages, wounded friendships, and led to destruction of many kinds. Up until now, our "Fun" weeks have centered around the importance of fun to the Christian life. This week, we're focusing on the boundaries we set for our fun.

What are your personal convictions in this area? Where has God led you to draw the line? What good fun are you thankful for? Where do you need to be careful in your fun?

APPLICATION QUESTIONS

1) How do you know when your fun has lapsed into something sinful—or at least unbeneficial?

2) What do you think the Israelites' reasons were for what they did? Can you sympathize with their frustrations at all? What could they have done instead of blaspheming God and worshiping an idol?

3) Think about your spheres of leadership. How might God want to use you as a good influence on those around you—to help them to enjoy healthy, God-honoring fun?

DECEMBER 17-23

WEEK 51

CHOOSE THIS DAY

Now therefore fear the Lord and serve him in sincerity and in faithfulness. Put away the gods that your fathers served beyond the River and in Egypt, and serve the Lord. And if it is evil in your eyes to serve the Lord, choose this day whom you will serve, whether the gods your fathers served in the region beyond the River, or the gods of the Amorites in whose land you dwell. But as for me and my house, we will serve the Lord.

—JOSHUA 24:14-15 (ESV)

THIS IS A GREAT segue from last week. Joshua was Moses' successor. He'd seen the Israelites doubt God again and again, resulting in forty years of wandering in the wilderness before they could enter the Promised Land. Now, Joshua exhorts them to choose once and for all. God has done amazing wonders for His people, sustaining and providing for them, rescuing and loving them. They have a choice to make.

We can't serve two masters (Matthew 6:24). A divided allegiance is meaningless to God. We have to make a choice. Maybe you're struggling in your faith or you've encountered a season where multiple things are pulling at your attention. Maybe the thought of being completely sold-out for God is intimidating, because you're not 100 percent sure that the Christian life is all it's cracked up to be. Maybe there's even a sliver of doubt in your mind that God exists!

We all experience these doubts sometimes. The important thing isn't never faltering in your faith—it's being dedicated to believing, even when you struggle to do so (Mark 9:24). We need to make up our minds about who we believe God is and live accordingly. Will we trust in what His Word says? Or will we wander around, trying to find the truth on our own?

James 2 tells us that true faith shows itself in our works. We don't work to earn salvation, but true salvation will show up in the works that God brings about in us through His Holy Spirit. Works are the evidence of our faith. Joshua is exhorting the children of Israel here to "put their money where their mouth is," in a sense. If they truly trust God, they need to live for Him. The same is true for us.

If we serve someone else or trust someone else in the place of God—giving them our ultimate allegiance, trusting in them to be our everything—then our faith probably isn't alive or genuine. True faith will show itself through works. So, whom will you serve?

APPLICATION QUESTIONS

1) What's the difference between working to try to earn faith and works being a result of faith?

2) What other forces or names are vying for your worship in the world today? Do you struggle to avoid replacing God with any of these? Explain your answer.

3) If someone claims to believe in God but looks nothing like God—if their works don't back up their belief—what might you conclude about that person?

DECEMBER 24-31

WEEK 52

A HEAVENLY FAMILY

For the Lord your God is the God of gods and the Lord of lords, the great, the mighty, and the awesome God, who does not show partiality, nor take a bribe. He executes justice for the orphan and the widow, and shows His love for the stranger by giving him food and clothing. So show your love for the stranger, for you were strangers in the land of Egypt.

—DEUTERONOMY 10:17-19 (NASB)

WE'VE EXPLORED FAMILY relationships this year in depth, but what about those who have no blood family? God commands His people to care for the outcast, the abandoned, and those without support. God shares what He is like with His people in this passage: how He has a heart for those who are hurting and lonely. Then, He requires the same of His people—since we've been shown compassion and unconditional love by God, we are to extend the same to those in our communities who are in need.

How can we support those without family? There are a myriad ways, but the simplest is getting to know your community better. There are likely organizations, shelters, and programs that will allow you to support orphans, widows, and others like them. Whether you do this financially, relationally, or by volunteering, the heart is the same: you're serving those who don't have all the connections and blessings that you have. And really, hasn't God done the same for you? He came to each one of us when we were spiritually dead—when we had nothing to offer Him—and He invited us into His family. Through Jesus' finished work on the cross, we have the opportunity to be adopted into God's family (Ephesians 1:5). How amazing is that?

Our hearts should respond to this incredible love with enthusiasm to share it with everyone—*especially* those who don't have an earthly family to reflect the love of the Father. This may seem intimidating, especially if your nature isn't to go out of your way to meet people or make connections. But start simple. Do some research. Get to know those in your community. Ask around at church about those who need meals cooked, a car ride somewhere, or simply someone to come keep them company every now and then. There may be a single mother who needs help, a young man who's looking for a father figure in his life, or any number of other people who need your support.

How can you show those around you the love of your Heavenly Father? How can you show them what the family of God looks like in action?

APPLICATION QUESTIONS

1) What do you think makes it so difficult for us to step out and help those closest to us geographically?

2) Read James 2:14-17. Again, we don't do works to earn salvation, but if a believer doesn't care at all for the poor, what might this reveal about his or her faith?

3) What's one concrete step you can take this week to move towards the needy and lonely in your community? Commit to taking that step, and ask God to encourage and empower you as you do.

www.ingramcontent.com/pod-product-compliance
Lightning Source LLC
Chambersburg PA
CBHW070049100426
42734CB00040B/2819